Libraries
ReadLearnConnect

THIS BOOK IS PART OF
ISLINGTON READS BOOKSWAP
SCHEME

Please take this book and either return it to a Bookswap site or replace with one of your own books that you would like to share.

If you enjoy this book, why not join your local Islington Library and borrow more like it for free?

Find out about our FREE e-book, e-audio, newspaper and magazine apps, activities for pre-school children and other services we have to offer at www.islington.gov.uk/libraries

ISLINGTON
For a more equal future

KEY THEMES IN POLICING

Series summary: This textbook series is designed to fill a growing need for titles which reflect the importance of incorporating 'evidence-based policing' within Higher Education curriculums. It will reflect upon the changing landscape of contemporary policing as it becomes more politicised, professionalised and scrutinised, and draw out both changes and continuities in its themes.

Series Editors: Megan O'Neill, University of Dundee, Marisa Silvestri, University of Kent and Stephen Tong, Canterbury Christ Church University

Forthcoming

Police Occupational Culture: Research and Practice – Tom Cockcroft, March 2020

Critical Perspectives on Police Leadership – Claire Davis and Marisa Silvestri, March 2020

Towards Ethical Policing – Dominic Wood, April 2020

Practical Psychology for Policing – Jason Roach, March 2021

Published

Miscarriages of Justice: Causes, Consequences and Remedies – Sam Poyser, Angus Nurse and Rebecca Milne, May 2018

Key Challenges in Criminal Investigation – Martin O'Neill, February 2018

Plural Policing: Theory and Practice – Colin Rogers, November 2016

Understanding Police Intelligence Work – Adrian James, April 2016

Editorial advisory board
Paul Quinton, College of Policing
Nick Fyfe, University of Dundee
Jennifer Brown, London School of Economics
Charlotte E. Gill, George Mason University

POLICING THE POLICE

Challenges of Democracy and Accountability

Michael Rowe

First published in Great Britain in 2020 by

Policy Press
University of Bristol
1-9 Old Park Hill
Bristol
BS2 8BB
UK
t: +44 (0)117 954 5940
pp-info@bristol.ac.uk
www.policypress.co.uk

North America office:
Policy Press
c/o The University of Chicago Press
1427 East 60th Street
Chicago, IL 60637, USA
t: +1 773 702 7700
f: +1 773-702-9756
sales@press.uchicago.edu
www.press.uchicago.edu

© Policy Press 2020

British Library Cataloguing in Publication Data
A catalogue record for this book is available from the British Library

Library of Congress Cataloging-in-Publication Data
A catalog record for this book has been requested

978-1-4473-4800-9 hardback
978-1-4473-4705-7 paperback
978-1-4473-4706-4 ePub
978-1-4473-4708-8 ePDF

Cover design by Andrew Corbett
Front cover image: istock
Printed and bound in Great Britain by CMP, Poole
Policy Press uses environmentally responsible print partners

Contents

List of abbreviations

AI	Artificial Intelligence
ANPR	Automatic Number Plate Recognition
APCC	Association of Police Crime Commissioners
APP	Authorised Professional Practice
BCU	Basic Command Unit
BSIA	British Security Industry Authority
BWC	Body Worn Camera
CDA	Crime and Disorder Act 1998
EBP	Evidence Based Policing
GIS	Geographic Information System
GMPA	Greater Manchester Police Authority
HAC	Home Affairs Committee
HMIC	Her Majesty's Inspector of Constabulary
HMICFRS	Her Majesty's Inspectorate of Constabulary and Fire and Rescue Services
IOPC	Independent Office for Police Conduct
IPCC	Independent Police Complaints Commission
IPSA	International Private Security Association
NCA	National Crime Agency
NIPB	Northern Ireland Policing Board
OSC	Office of Surveillance Commissioners
PACE	Police and Criminal Evidence Act 1984
PALG	Police Action Lawyers Group
PCC	Police and Crime Commissioner
PCP	Police and Crime Panels
PSD	Professional Standards Department
PSNI	Police Service of Northern Ireland
SOCO	Scene of Crime Officer
SPA	Scottish Police Authority

Series preface

Megan O'Neill, Marisa Silvestri and Stephen Tong

The *Key Themes in Policing* series aims to provide relevant and useful books to support the growing number of policing modules on both undergraduate and postgraduate programmes. The series also aims to support all those interested in policing, from criminology, law and policing students to policing professionals and those who wish to join policing services. It also seeks to respond to the call for evidence-based policing led by organisations such as the College of Policing in England and Wales. By producing a range of high-quality, research-informed texts on important areas in policing, contributions to the series support and inform both professional and academic policing curriculums.

Representing the fifth publication in the series, *Policing the Police: Challenges of Democracy and Accountability*, by Michael Rowe, explores fundamental issues concerning how the police are governed. In recent years, the police have experienced substantial structural changes in terms, the introduction of Police and Crime Commissioners (now in their second term), and the nationalisation of policing in Scotland; financial restraint with austerity and funding cutbacks; rising demand; increased pluralisation of policing providers; and evolving technological change presenting new and complex challenges for organisations and practitioners. This book provides an excellent insight into how the police are governed and the challenges occurring during this time of rapid change in policing in the UK.

Michael Rowe is a Professor of Criminology at the University of Northumbria. Michael has published widely on policing matters over a long period of time, with specific interests in police culture and reforms, police accountability and ethics, race and racism, and the policing of domestic violence. Michael is a regular contributor to policing debates across the world and has been a member of the Executive of the British Society of Criminology and Vice-President of the Australian and New Zealand Society of Criminology. He was an academic member of the Independent Police Commission chaired by Lord Stevens in 2010. Michael is extremely well placed to deliver a publication focusing on democratic policing and the challenges of accountability which serves as an important source to inform discussions about democracy and accountability as it relates to policing now and in the future. The book is valuable in reflecting on the evolving role of police and governance in a rapidly changing world and will be a key text for anyone interested in policing.

Preface

This book has been a long time in the making, and the writing of it has given me a welcome opportunity to revisit and rethink debates and discussions encountered previously in many different contexts. Given that, a list of acknowledgements is not provided; I'd forget to include people and so have opted to risk mildly offending lots of people, rather than seriously offending a few. It is up to you, dear reader, to decide if this is a cowardly or a utilitarian decision.

I would like specifically to thank the editors of the series, who invited this book and have provided welcome feedback on the initial proposal and at various points along the way. Similarly, an anonymous reviewer has helped guide me along the path, and I am grateful for their advice. Stuart Lister and Kevin Morrell have provided insight into particular chapters and helped shaped my thoughts around accountability and emerging challenges in relation to evidence-based and big data policing.

The book is dedicated with much love to my parents, Lis and Ken Rowe.

Police accountability in the 21st century: new wine, new bottles?

The 21st century poses distinct new twists for the very long-standing challenge of holding police to account and providing democratic governance of a range of law enforcement and regulatory agencies with considerable power over citizens. Web-based technology and artificial intelligence (AI) seem poised to transform policing and social regulation in fundamental ways just as swathes of other industries and services have experienced. Often characterised as 'predictive policing', the possibility that law enforcement and partner agencies might mine vast reserves of intelligence and data in order to forecast – with spectacular accuracy – the perpetrator, venue and timing of offences yet to happen offers a policing future by turns terrifying and exhilarating in criminological terms. Potentially, the reach of such technologies expands the scope and power of policing such that long-established moral, ethical and political concerns about democratic accountability are considerably more pressing. By 2020 the Chinese government plans to have fully deployed a social credit system that uses big data and principles of commercial credit scoring to assess the 'trustworthiness' and social standing of all citizens, using vast and complex systems of surveillance technology (Liang et al 2018). Not only does this new combination of policing, surveillance and regulation offer the possibility of identifying any individual anywhere in China within a matter of moments, it provides the basis for high-level social sorting such that freedom of movement, access to services, and political and social participation can be permitted or denied via technological assemblages. It is argued at many points in the book that the rush to technological determinism needs to be resisted in the face of such predictions: that such developments might be technically possible does not mean that they will be enacted. In liberal democratic societies, civil, legal and political conventions could provide important resistance to the developments predicted in China. These mechanisms seem to be particular dystopian in the context of a totalitarian regime with scant regard for human rights – and in which democratic governance of policing is absent – but the extension of similar principles and practices begins to extend to western liberal democracies and so raises new challenges in terms of how the guards are guarded. The emerging problem for governance is not just that big data 'predictive policing' is more pervasive and intensive than the policing systems operating when current arrangements for accountability were devised – although that is part of the problem. What makes the challenge more significant is that these policing formations are deployed by new constellations of government agencies, private corporations, and a new cadre of technicians, business people and scientists – many operating in a global network outwith the oversight of national oversight agencies. Some of the products – the databases and software – created by these new policing systems are 'self-learning' and autonomous, making it difficult to interrogate and regulate future unknown bases of decision making.

Policing the police becomes a more complex challenge as this technological transformation tests the capacity of principles and mechanisms for governance and accountability established (at least in England and Wales) in the mid-19th century. Other foundational shifts have also moved the terrain of police governance, particularly in relation to the increasing role of private and third-party agencies in the delivery of policing. Regulation of policing activity can no longer (if ever it could) be considered solely or largely in terms of holding police officers and constabularies to account. For decades, scholars have focused attention on the expanding role of private security companies in the delivery of policing (Shearing and Stenning 1981; Johnston 1992; White 2012) and more recently, focus has extended further to include a new conglomeration of agencies from public, private and third sectors engaged in a wide range of regulatory activity. Banks, health services, universities, private landlords and employers have become responsibilised in an age of security such that they are legally required to verify the identity and activity of citizens. Brodeur (2007) argued that the surveillance of citizens traditionally conducted by 'high' policing agencies of the state has extended, post 9/11, to inform 'low' policing, and it can be argued that there has been horizontal as well as vertical integration such that a plethora of 'non-police' organisations have been incorporated into such activity. As is outlined later in the book, some of these agencies and some of these activities are subject to regulation of various kinds, but these provisions tend not to be incorporated into more general provisions for police governance. The private security industry in Britain, for example, is subject to legal and professional regulation but this is not integrated into arrangements for the governance of policing, even though such companies can play significant roles in the delivery of policing in many forms. This book seeks to extend analysis of policing the police through considering the implications of new networks, including multinational partners, in the delivery of policing. It is argued that established arrangements of governance tend to be focused on institutions of policing and as such are not well placed to address practices and power emerging from relationships among and between complex webs of providers.

A third set of challenges – in addition to technological changes and the pluralisation of policing – is similarly often overlooked in discussion of police governance. Passing any judgement – positively or negatively – about the effectiveness of the governance of policing entails, even if only implicitly, an assumption that there is some normative consensus or benchmark against which a particular action or outcome can be measured. To argue, for example, that a police officer acted with unnecessary violence against a member of the public requires that there is some shared understanding as to what degree of violence might have been legitimate. A claim that the policing of a particular crime is effective requires some view as to what constitutes an 'effective' response: is this that the crime is never committed, or that offenders are usually caught, or that victims tend to be satisfied with the police response? These are micro-level illustrations of a more fundamental challenge of identifying the appropriate mandate for policing. Crime control is usually central to defining the mandate (and the one to which politicians and the media often return [Loader 2014]), but it is widely established that the public police perform a wide repertoire of roles that have little or no link to law enforcement. Service roles, the maintenance of order and – more recently – a commitment to protecting vulnerable people and communities – offer alternative perspectives on the fundamental question of the purpose of policing. It is argued in more detail later in this text that there is a declining basis for consensus as to the appropriate mandate for policing in the face of increasing economic inequalities and social and political marginalisation. Neoliberal individualism in western societies has promoted a consumerist culture such that citizens are made responsible for their own security, but the grounds for collective provision or consensus are undermined. It is argued later that the problem identified by Bowling and Sheptycki (2012) in relation to global policing – that it is difficult to locate a set of collective norms and values that could develop a global civic society to provide for accountability – seems increasing likely to apply within nation states characterised by high levels of division and inequality. Through considering changing problems in terms of 'the public', community and consensus, this book also broadens the critical approach to the challenge of police governance and argues that focusing on institutional and legal arrangements threatens to overlook difficulties of identifying the 'ends' that police governance seeks to fulfil.

The central themes of this book – exploring how policing is governed and held to account in complex contemporary societies – cover ground that is well established but also emerging and cutting edge. To adapt the old adage, there are both 'new wines and new bottles' evident in contemporary debates. As is shown in later chapters, the central preoccupations of political philosophers remain highly pertinent to considerations of how 21st-century globalised societies can 'guard the guards'. Central to this is the tacit social contract that free individuals in liberal democratic societies delegate responsibility to the state and afford to the police the right to exercise power, enforce the law and apply the legitimate use of force against those free individuals. This gives rise to the fundamental political problem of how to ensure that the agencies afforded this power over the public are to be regulated such that their unique position is not abused. Much of what follows is a reflection on how these principles can and should be applied to policing services in an era when 'modern' police services, first instigated in the 19th century, are hugely transformed. To these long-standing debates are added distinctly new challenges emerging from a technological revolution that promises (or threatens?) to transform the organisation and delivery of policing. Similarly, and relatedly, globalisation shapes new crime problems and challenges in ways that provide new agendas, such as the migration of human beings and capital, or climate change, for law enforcement to meet, as well as new formations of policing that themselves transcend national boundaries and so raise new challenges of governance. Shifts within many nation states have extended opportunities for private policing agencies and created environments in which a range of organisations – from public, private and 'third' sectors – are required to regulate the behaviour of citizens, clients, residents, customers, students, patients and the wider public in ways not previously part of their operational activity. Questions about police and policing require consideration of the role of a host of organisations that would not have featured in debates even just a decade or so ago.

Structure of the book

The book begins by analysing accountability in terms of traditional approaches. First, in terms of the formal arrangements for governance and direction, and second, in terms of diverse mechanisms in place to scrutinise service delivery, investigate complaints and respond to areas of performance regarded as problematic. These two Janus-faced elements comprise the 'hard' modes of accountability: they are formalised in law and regulation, rely on investigatory powers delivered by dedicated staff, have codified powers of sanctioning, and are exclusive in terms of focus on delivering accountability.

Where the book extends analysis is by arguing that an increasing range of wider activities can be considered as 'soft' instruments that might deliver similar outcomes. Taking up Reiner's (1985: 296) point that 'all discussions of police policy and reform eventually lead to the fundamental issue of police accountability', it is argued that anything that seeks to influence the exercise of police officer discretion can be considered as a form of regulation and governance. As is outlined in the second chapter of this book, it is the central and inevitable role of discretion in policing that makes the principle of accountability so difficult and so significant. Given the legitimate capacity of police to use force against citizens and to intervene in ways that restrict their rights, and that decisions to do this are highly contextual and impossible to pre-configure, the nature of a host of managerial and professional practices, and influences of external observers and agencies, can be considered as potential forms of accountability.

Further to this, the book considers the possibilities that some current policing strategies might have in terms of democratic oversight. Although moves towards Evidence Based Policing (EBP) or authorised practice are not usually explored in terms of accountability, the book argues that in theory and in application, both offer models for directing officers since discretion and autonomy are delimited. The principle that policing ought to be delivered on the basis of scientific research or in keeping with a code of ethical practice has the potential to direct officers into certain forms of action or modes of delivery. Both approaches also raise questions about the extent to which policing ought to be delivered in terms of democratic demands, even if those are not evidence-based or consistent with integrity statements. This raises the challenge as whether policing in broad terms should be assessed in normative terms, or if technical scientific standards can provide a benchmark. Finally, technological change in the form of the use of big data, crime mapping, intelligence systems and the like, are considered as a form of 'soft power' that can direct and control police behaviour and provide retrospective accountability of police interventions.

Contemporary developments relating to EBP are critiqued on the basis that little attention has been paid to the impact of diverse forms of accountability on policing. While there is important research evidence on the link between public perceptions of police procedural justice and legitimacy, there remains little wider research into ways in which 'hard' mechanisms impact on police service delivery, operational effectiveness, or leadership and management. Some of the emerging work on Police and Crime Commissioners (PCCs) gives some insight, but this is nascent, and the impact of other formal systems on the general mandate is limited.

These broad themes and debates are explored throughout the chapters that follow. This and the following chapter, as outlined below, establish the conceptual framework applied throughout the rest of the book. Issues of accountability and governance are defined in general terms and classical political philosophical approaches to the 'guarding of the guards' problem are reviewed. A model of accountability developed by Romzek and Dubnick (1987) distinguishes between the 'hard' and 'soft', and 'internal' and 'external', dimensions that are applied as an organising framework throughout the rest of the text, and the model is introduced in Chapter 2. The following two chapters (3 and 4) review established mechanisms and institutional arrangements for police governance and accountability. Further to that, a series of chapters (5, 6 and 7) consider new and emerging challenges, some of which were outlined earlier in this introduction. These include the implications of big data and EBP as new modes of delivery and strategic approaches to policing which might offer considerable improvements in terms of efficiency and the enhancing of professional delivery, but which nonetheless raise significant questions about democratic governance. Chapter 8 reviews the underlying conclusions and challenges that emerge throughout the book. In particular, it is argued that changing political economy and the declining power of the nation state in a global environment combine to weaken established mechanisms of accountability. Moreover, the same processes decrease the possibility of creating social consensus in relation to the proper mandate and value of democratic policing. It is argued that fundamental attention to tackling marginalisation and inequality are vital if effective democratic oversight of policing is to be achieved.

Chapter 2 draws on public administration, legal and political science literature, and establishes some of the conceptual framework necessary to understand 'accountability', including the vexed notion of operational independence and the empirical evidence supporting the importance of legitimacy for effective practice. Different forms and practices of accountability are outlined and it is argued that the complexity and difficulty of defining the term needs to be recognised, since distinct forms and ends are reviewed in later chapters. The model of accountability introduced by Romzek and Dubnick (1987) that establishes a four-way distinction between 'hard' and 'soft', and 'internal' and 'external' approaches is reviewed since this provides an organising framework for the different levels and dimensions assessed in this text.

Chapter 3 explores the governance and politics of policing. Multi-level governance of policing provides a range of statutory mechanisms to hold public police to account, and the applicability of these models to contemporary policing is considered. Democratic policing is analysed in principle and in practice with reference to the four nations of the UK, other European countries, the US and Australasia. In the UK context, the various roles of central government, PCCs, devolved and local government and agencies such as Her Majesty's Inspectorate of Constabulary are critically analysed. It is argued in this chapter that the conventional distinction between local and national forms of governance, in England and Wales at least, continues to provide a useful way of conceptualising arrangements but does not easily accommodate emerging provisions that cut across these boundaries.

Chapter 4 is focused on the significant and widespread challenges associated with investigating complaints and discipline. Established civil, criminal and legal routes that provide formal mechanisms for remedies and restitutions following police misconduct are reviewed. New data on trends in civil claims against police in England and Wales provides evidence to suggest that this remains a limited avenue for addressing wrongdoing. Impressionistically, at least, it seems that the adequacy of all complaints provisions is questioned in most liberal democratic societies, and efforts to provide robust, external and independent investigations are explored. In relation to England and Wales it is noted that a trend towards greater transparency in the response to alleged misconduct has been regarded as a means of securing greater trust and confidence in the system. Links between these provisions and the College of Policing Code of Ethics, which offers a different approach to improving officer conduct, are critically reviewed. Given the wider emphasis on pluralisation of policing, Chapter 4 includes discussion on the legal, social and political measures that might provide some oversight of private security.

Chapter 5 critically explores the growing recognition and promotion of science, evidence and police accountability in the age of big data. It is argued that the use of scientific evidence to develop improved policing services offers many advantages, and that EBP is a valuable means of promoting professionalisation for the public police. Nonetheless, it is argued in this chapter that these developments are inherently concerned with reorienting police behaviour and practice, and their growing significance in contemporary policing means that it is of vital importance to consider the implications that they have in terms of democratic accountability and public oversight. Several examples are used to illustrate circumstances where policing outcomes shaped by science and the 'evidence base' have been in tension with public expectation and demand. Although not centrally considered as means of regulation and governance, EBP and big data are addressed as 'soft' forms of accountability.

Similarly, Chapter 6 considers other dimensions of internal management and leadership. Modalities and technologies of police leadership and management are considered in this chapter as 'soft' forms of accountability in the sense that while they are not intended as mechanisms of regulation and governance they nonetheless have influence in such terms. Research on the impact of ethics and integrity programmes indicates how these often intend to promote forms of officer behaviour and decision making, and so to delimit unfettered office discretion. This is a form of accountability. So, too, the promotion of diversity within policing and cultural transformation is (among other things) heralded as a way of enhancing decision making, again a method of shaping officer behaviour.

Chapter 7 focuses on external oversight of policing by the public through de-centred and unorganised activities associated with social media and online technology. As in other fields, the scope and capacity of 'citizen journalism' to monitor and reveal malfeasance among police is considered in relation to a number of high-profile international examples. From police involvement in fatal shootings in the US to more mundane footage of excessive force or apparent misconduct, there have been in recent years numerous examples of members of the public recording and disseminating footage that has held police to account in ways previously unimaginable. The chapter questions the extent to which the external gaze on officers really offers a brave new world in which public scrutiny is a powerful mechanism of accountability. Not least of the problems outlined is that the independent free spaces of social media are disconnected from any formal mechanisms of accountability. Principles of justice, equity and due process do not apply and so capacity is limited by the extent to which individual cases of wrongdoing can gather attention in the maelstrom of social media. White (2016) rightly notes that 'critical public discourse' can be a mechanism for holding private security companies to account, and this model is critically applied in this chapter to the potential for social media to perform a similar role for policing.

Chapter 8 concludes the book by analysing challenges of police governance in relation to processes of social inequality, neoliberal individualism and police pluralisation and globalisation. It is argued that greater attention needs to be paid to the changing context in which mechanisms developed (broadly) alongside the modern police in the 19th century currently operate. Key among these are arguments that the position of the nation state – the sovereign source of accountability in traditional models – is weakened in relation to transnational and networked policing (Wood and Shearing 2007). Not only has this process meant that power (and so the subject of accountability) been de-territorialised, it has also meant that private and third-sector agencies have become embedded into practices of policing and regulation such that these become much more difficult to hold to account. As Wood and Shearing (2007) note, power increasingly resides in the relationships between the nodes in this networked environment, and not in the nodes themselves. The other main focus of the chapter takes the point made by Bowling and Sheptycki (2012) that a challenge for meaningful accountability of transnational policing is that there is not a coherent 'demos' or set of normative standards against which accountability can be applied. The chapter argues, following Reiner (2007), that this trend is true within the nation state and that neoliberal individualism has brought the 'end of consensus'. This might explain why private or citizen-led mechanisms of accountability (for example, civil action against police) seem to have overtaken traditional public responses. These are not just preferred avenues for technical or financial reasons, but also representative of a decline in the possibility of *public* oversight of police work.

Further reading

Rawlings, P. (2005) *Policing: A Short History*. Cullompton: Willan.
Reiner, R. (2007) *Law and Order: An Honest Citizen's Guide to Crime and Control*. Cambridge: Polity.
Vitale, A. (2017) *The End of Policing*. London: Verso Books.

2

Principles and purposes
of accountability

Drawing on public administration, legal and political science literature, this chapter establishes some of the conceptual framework necessary to understand police accountability, including the vexed notion of operational independence and the empirical evidence supporting the importance of legitimacy for effective practice. At the end of the chapter is a discussion of the changing nature of police governance in neoliberal globalised societies in which state-centred models of governance are increasingly strained. Pluralised and networked forms of policing, engaging agencies across sectors and across national borders, appear difficult to hold to account and the possibility of ensuring democratic policing, responsive to the needs and interests of the public, seems ever more difficult to secure. It is noted throughout the chapter that the ends of accountability are varied, and are important as a matter of principle as well as practical effectiveness. In the following chapter the discussion develops to consider the operationalisation of accountability through organisational practices at national and local level, and in relation to pluralised policing.

That the police in modern liberal democratic society ought to be accountable to political authorities, and ultimately to the public at large, is a straightforward principle in as much as all public institutions are governed by the local and national state, and networks of 'arms-length' regulators, inspectors and auditors. The principles and practices of public administration extend to the police alongside other public services; indeed a classic early study of the role and power of police constables over citizens identified officers as 'street level bureaucrats' (Lipsky 1980). This study cast police officers as equivalent to other public officials, such as social workers or educationalists, since all have considerable discretionary powers to interpret and enforce public policy in ways that directly impact on the life chances of their clients.

In other regards, however, police agencies stand apart from other public sector institutions in ways that raise significant issues of power and so raise important questions of accountability. Symbolically and in practice, the police embody the sovereign state and have the recourse to use legitimate force against citizens in ways rarely available to other public bodies. In the 1970s, while he was Commissioner of the Metropolitan Police, Sir Robert Mark claimed that the duties of the police far outweighed their powers and that the only significant power that they held over fellow citizens was the 'power to inconvenience them' (Judge 1986: 175). In narrow legal terms Mark might have been correct, but his analysis overlooked the significant cultural, organisational and social dimensions that distinguish police powers from those of other public and private bodies. Few other agencies have the legitimate authority to ask citizens to – among other things – account for themselves, to enter and search private property, to detain members of the public and to restrict entry into public spaces. In liberal democratic societies that claim to guarantee the rights and freedom of citizens and to protect them against encroachment by the state, the position of the police service seems, to put it mildly, anomalous. Loader and Walker (2007: 205) identified this as the 'central paradox' of state policing, that as the 'monopolist of coercive resources the police stand simultaneously as the guarantor of, and threat to, citizen security'. The police are able to countermand the freedom of the citizen and can be the agency that encroaches on behalf of the state, and are required to perform such roles legitimately and with the consent of the public. Reiner (2013) referred to this anomaly as the 'riddle' of police accountability, which he characterised in the following terms: 'Relying on any agents to deal with deviance or preserve peace potentially leads to an infinite redress. Who or what protects against the guards' deviance or unreliability? And then how is that line of security itself secured, and so on – a potentially infinite regress.'

Social contract political theorists suggest that the way through this conundrum is to conceptualise a tacit bargain between the citizen and the state. Hobbes, Locke and Rousseau conceived of human beings in a state of nature and that the roots of the state stemmed from an implicit bargain such that each person surrenders a portion of their individual sovereignty to a state, which, in return, offers them security. The Hobbesian bargain provides for a central powerful state, a Leviathan able to ensure the avoidance of the 'war of all against all' that would otherwise characterise human relations. Arising from this bargain – in legal, administrative and philosophical terms – are questions about the nature of this settlement, the limits and conditions surrounding the power of the state relative to the citizen, and the mechanisms required to ensure that the delicate balance is maintained. Jos (2006) argued that social contract theory continues to offer a potential basis for the legitimacy of public administration, including policing, as will be developed further below. Police power and authority is devolved from the state – legally, financially and symbolically – such that the police embody sovereignty, the police are the 'state in uniform'. On this basis, questions of the power of the state relative to citizens transfer to debates about the power of the police over the public and the safeguards imposed to prevent the abuse of those powers.

That the rights and powers of police over citizens ought to be limited, subject to the rule of law and authored by the state on behalf of the public at large forms the starting point for formal 'hard' practices of police accountability. Before considering the practices through which this principle has been realised, which is the focus of Chapter 3, it is worthwhile reviewing some key terms and concepts, and that is the focus of the discussion that follows in this chapter.

The centrality of discretion to policing

A central reason why police accountability is both challenging and necessary is that individual police officers have considerable scope to exercise discretion as they go about their duties. As noted, Lipsky (1980) argued that this was a characteristic shared with other public servants, but in the context of police work the exercise of discretion is particularly charged since it may entail decisions with greater significance in terms of public safety, liberty and freedom, and may entail the use of physical force. Unlike other public agencies, police might be *obliged* to use violence against fellow citizens in the proper discharge of their duties (Westley 1953) – and individual officers are responsible for how they exercise their discretion in the application of their powers. The recognition that junior ranks are required to interpret their legal powers and apply these selectively has been a recurring preoccupation of police studies since the early 1960s. Important early work in terms of modern research and analysis of policing includes that of Joseph Goldstein (1960) and Herman Goldstein (1964), who distinguished between the 'law in books' and the 'law in practice' and demonstrated that police officers, working in conditions of low visibility beyond the scope of line managers, had considerable autonomy when it came to deciding whether or how to apply the law. Decisions not to apply the law at all ('to turn a blind eye') are particularly difficult for managers to interrogate since, by definition, they result in no action and no record. The 'discovery' of police discretion through early sociological studies of policing in the 1960s and 1970s led to debates as to whether police officers were overreaching their constitutional role of applying the law and adopting 'quasi-judicial functions' (Neyroud and Beckley 2001: 82).

Discretion is inherent to policing for practical and ethical reasons: since police resources are limited, and for many years (in the UK at least), decreasing in real terms, there is inevitably the need to create priorities. Furthermore, even if certain crime or social problems are judged to be priority tasks, individual officers still have to decide how to respond: from ignoring a specific misdemeanour, to 'words of advice', to a conditional caution of some type, through to an arrest. For ethical reasons too, it would be unreasonable for police to apply the maximum letter of the law without consideration of the particular circumstances of an individual case. As Reiner (2000: 169) noted, 'even the most precisely worded rule of law requires interpretation in concrete situations'. None of that is particularly problematic, *providing* that police officers exercise that discretion in a manner that is consistent with the established policies, procedures, guidelines, codes, laws and norms prevalent more broadly across society. It is the complexity of that proviso that is the focus of much of the remainder of this book.

Models of accountability

The term 'accountability' is used in multiple ways, and often without any clear reflection on what it means. As Bovens (2007: 448) noted, accountability 'is one of those golden concepts that no one can be against. It is increasingly used in political discourse and policy documents because it conveys an image of transparency and trustworthiness'. More succinctly, Reiner (2016: 134) stated that accountability is a 'weasel word'. The term derives from the obvious near synonym of accounting, as developed following the Norman Conquest of 1066 when William I conducted a 'count' of property, income and population, as catalogued in the Domesday Book, for the purpose of raising tax revenue (Dubnick 2002, cited in Bovens 2007). Many of the systems for police accountability developed in recent years demonstrate that this financial model of accountability continues to apply, although the concept has clearly broadened considerably to embrace a wider range of formats and outcomes. The logic and focus of accountability are varied, including ensuring that public funds are used 'efficiently and effectively'. Formally this is the focus of Her Majesty's Inspector's annual inspection of each police service, which is required to certify that these two outcomes are achieved and Home Office funding can continue to be provided. As this book demonstrates, though, there is a considerable range of organisations formally charged with overseeing aspects of police activity. The ends of this oversight are many and various, including to ensure officers do not abuse their powers, that police meet local priorities, that workforce management complies with equal opportunities legislation, that criminal justice processes are properly enacted, that established ethical and normative standards are met, that public confidence and police legitimacy are nurtured, and that police equipment and vehicles meet required standards – of course this is not an exhaustive list and there is considerable overlap between some of these elements. Jarvis (2014) outlined a four-fold model of accountability and suggested that the various purposes to which it is directed could be organised into key central ideas (Jarvis 2014: 453):

- Democratic: 'accountability controls and legitimizes government actions by linking them to "democratic chain of delegation"'.
- Assurance: 'accountability is essential to withstand the tendency toward power concentration and abuse of powers in the executive branch'.
- Learning: 'accountability provides public office-holders and agencies with feedback-based inducements to increase their effectiveness and efficiency'.
- Results: 'accountability concentrates focus on ensuring that public resources are utilized to secure desired public policy outcomes'.

Useful though this schema is in terms of navigating through the complexities of police accountability in the 21st century it does not resolve some of the fundamental challenges that will be returned to in the chapters that follow. Challenges can be identified in relation to each of the four dimensions. Suggestions that the capacity and viability of nation states are undermined in a globalised world call into question the extent to which a 'democratic chain of delegation' is a credible mechanism in the context of 'networked policing' (Wood and Shearing 2007) in which private and transnational agencies are joined with local or national police services. In terms of the second dimension, the value of accountability in terms of preventing power becoming excessively concentrated is limited when social, political and economic inequalities within societies fracture mutual bonds and exacerbate criminogenic conditions that mean that problems of crime and disorder bear more heavily on disadvantaged communities (Wilkinson and Pickett 2009). Mechanisms for police accountability might prevent police becoming unduly powerful but they do little to address the wider inequalities in power that determine the social context in which policing is delivered. Similarly, critical reflection on the role of science and research in the development of EBP suggests that policing is not always an environment in which learning opportunities to improve future performance are grasped (Telep and Somers 2017). Fourthly, while accountability is central to procedural justice that enhances public confidence in policing (Bradford 2014), as discussed further below, it is less clear that there is consensus in relation to the 'desired public policy outcomes' associated with policing. These and other concerns about police accountability are developed subsequently in this book.

The plethora of formal oversight agencies adds to the complexity of understanding the value and purpose of accountability. In the previous chapter a distinction was drawn between 'hard' and 'soft' mechanisms of accountability. Focusing just on the 'hard' formal legal and organisational framework of police accountability, there is clearly a diverse range of actors networked in complex relationships operating internationally, nationally, regionally and locally and sometimes crossing sectoral boundaries. As a way of modelling complex systems of public accountability, Romzek and Dubnick (1987, cited in Chan and Rosenbloom 2010) suggested a four-way distinction between internal and external sources of control and between those with high and low degrees of control. In terms of forms of accountability internal to organisations they identified bureaucratic mechanisms as having high levels of control since they prioritise the demands of those at the top of the organisation and give them scope to supervise those below them. In formal terms the traditional arrangements for police discipline could be characterised in these terms. Secondly, they identify professional forms of accountability that are also internally sourced but which offer a low degree of control since they place responsibility in the hands of employees who are expected to operate in accordance with agreed standards. Some of the professional standards developed by the College of Policing might be thought of in these terms. The third system of accountability is external control exercised through legal channels, which offer high levels of control where they are enforced by criminal sanctions. The work of the Independent Office for Police Conduct (IOPC) offers such legal control. Fourthly, Romzek and Dubnick (1987) outline external control exercised through political means, which might offer less overall control of the organisation when it is exercised by diverse external agents. In policing terms the complex oversight offered by the Home Office, PCCs, local authorities and MPs does not provide a coherent set of demands to which police have to respond.

The fuzzy boundaries of operational independence

Furthermore, senior police officers have significant political power of their own. This stems from the legal status of their office, the collective power and influence that chief officers wield through the National Police Chiefs' Council, and the cultural and symbolic power of senior officers as 'moral entrepreneurs' (Becker 1963). That senior officers themselves occupy positions of relative power and are somewhat able to resist external oversight and accountability leads to consideration of an important qualification that applies to the field of policing in ways not mirrored in other public services. The principle that policing is operationally independent from political interference is foundational in common law countries. As the literature on English police history demonstrates, opposition to the establishment of the Metropolitan Police, from the late 18th century, was based in part on fears that such an organisation would be akin to an internal militia in the command of an over-powerful central state. Orthodox police histories maintain that part of the 'genius' of the model developed by Home Secretary Peel was to placate such concerns by emphasising the independence of the new police in terms of operational law enforcement. The separation of powers such that local Watch Committees shared responsibility for funding police with central government, and chief constables were accountable only to the law in terms of operational matters provided the formal arrangement for police governance (Marshall 1965; Lustgarten 1986). The principle was reaffirmed in Lord Denning's 1968 judgment,[1] which stated that in operational matters police officers were answerable only to the law, a statement widely critiqued in terms of its representation of the legal position, but nonetheless a statement commonly cited as a core principle of policing in many common law countries (Stenning 2011; Reiner 2013). While the arrangements for police governance have changed – as much of this book, and Chapter 3 in particular, testifies – the principle of operational independence persists into the 21st century. The 2011 Policing Protocol Order outlined the power of, and relationship between, chief constables, the Home Secretary, PCCs and Police and Crime Panels and stipulated in Article 30:

> The operational independence of the police is a fundamental principle of British policing. It is expected by the Home Secretary that the professional discretion of the police service and oath of office give surety to the public that this shall not be compromised.

While operational independence might be a simple and elegant legal principle, it is apparent that in practice there is considerable and inherent ambiguity relating to the balance between police autonomy and oversight. Although these complexities have always surrounded policing, they have not impacted on all police organisations to the same degree. Prior to the 1964 Police Act there were differences in the legal status between chief officers of municipal and county police forces such that the former were expected to follow local direction to a greater extent than the latter. Municipal chief officers were required to act under the direction of the local Watch Committee (Reiner 1991), while the chief constables of county forces had considerable autonomy from other local government offices. This difference between the accountability of municipal and county forces reflected that the latter were part of local political and social elites, and often drawn from military and public school backgrounds much superior to chief officers of urban forces (Wall 1998). While in the 21st century it might be legally and constitutionally forbidden for PCCs, the Home Secretary or any other agency to direct the particular activities of officers as they enforce the law, there is a highly fuzzy boundary between that narrow preclusion and the arena in which it is the constitutional duty of political authorities to intervene. Resources available to police are set through the combined decisions of the Home Office and PCCs, who also determine the priorities that each local service ought to attend to. PCCs shape the local landscape of policing through commissioning victim and other services from private sector or voluntary agencies. They are also able to lever funding from central government and other agencies dedicated to particular priority areas and this will also shape the local policing agenda. All of this is properly within the scope and function of the PCC and none of this activity necessarily compromises operational independence directly in terms of how particular cases are policed, but they do configure the local context against which officer discretion is exercised.

Neither resourcing nor prioritising tasks inevitably influence the discretion enshrined in law to individual officers, but both clearly create a framework in which it is exercised. Acting entirely within their proper remit, a PCC might determine that roads policing ought to be a local priority and so work with the chief constable to develop detailed plans and ensure appropriate resources are available to deliver on them. None of that places any formal constraint on the operational independence of police officers but since laws are selectively enforced (as it would be neither possible nor desirable to enforce all laws all of the time) prioritisation of some tasks inevitably demotes others in the hierarchy of importance. As Lister (2013) noted, the external influence of political authorities on police activities is not necessarily normatively problematic in a democratic system in which the police should be responsive to public expectations, but it does indicate that operational independence is problematic in practice. Soon after the first PCCs took office in 2012 a series of cases tested the nature and extent of their power to dismiss chief officers. Following several controversies surrounding the propriety of PCCs dismissing chief officers the Home Affairs Committee (HAC) argued there were no effective checks to prevent a PCC sacking a Chief Constable even when their concerns were about operational policing (HAC 2013a). Clearly the days are gone when a chief constable could reflect, as an English Chief Constable had in his mid-20th-century memoirs, that 'in operational matters a Chief Constable is answerable to God, his Queen, his conscience, and to no one else' (Stenning 2011: 253).

A further confusion relating to the political independence of policing stems from the conflation and confusion of party politics and 'politics' in wider terms. Often the demand to 'keep politics out of policing' relates to the relatively narrow domain of party political activity. Officers in England and Wales are prohibited by the 2003 Police Regulations from joining extremist political parties, such as the British National Party, and the regulations and the College of Policing Code of Ethics stipulates that officers must not be actively involved in party politics more generally (although what 'actively involved' means is not clearly defined). Controversies about the politicisation of policing, such as the long-running saga of police engagement with the MP Damian Green, which culminated in 2017 with his sacking as Deputy Prime Minister following allegations made by former police officers and a 2008 raid on his parliamentary office, have revolved around the possibility that police have become involved in party politics in ways that might compromise the appearance of neutrality and independence. In the public row known as 'Plebgate' it was initially alleged that a government minister had demanded that officers open the gated entrance to Downing Street in order to let him cycle through (Westmarland and Rowe, 2018). When they refused it was alleged by the officers that the minster referred to them as 'fucking plebs'. This very brief exchange, and the language used, led to a political tussle that dragged on for months and was a lightning rod for conflict between government and police during the early years of austerity measures (Millie 2013). This was a problematic example of party political police engagement (although it was primarily the Police Federation, not police services themselves, that became embroiled in the row). Previously, concerns of a similar character had emerged in 2005 in relation to interventions by senior officers as politicians debated government proposals to extend the period during which individuals could be detained without charge. The role of the Association of Chief Police Officers in lobbying politicians on the need to support government proposals straddled the narrow line between the expression of professional opinion and party political advocacy. In the opposite direction, perhaps, the ability of politicians to compromise the independence of officers was demonstrated in relation to the resignations of Metropolitan Police Commissioners Blair and Stephenson, in 2005 and 2011 respectively, both of which followed public criticism by, in Blair's case, the Mayor of London, and, in respect of Stephenson, the Home Secretary. In neither case did the Commissioner leave their post following a formal process, as has happened in a number of instances involving PCCs – and which will be explored in Chapter 3 – but rather as a result of senior politicians expressing their lack of confidence and so making their position untenable.

All of these cases illustrate dimensions of 'soft' political power over the police and raise questions about the nature of media coverage and the broader political context in which governance operates. Arguably, none of the examples cited here unfolded in ways that correspond to formal processes or systems of accountability (the 'hard' powers). In each case they were determined, in part, by the prevailing political climate of the period: without post-Brexit factionalism within the Conservative government, for example, and the resignations of other senior figures, it is unlikely that the scandals surrounding Green would have been so significant and so the debate about the role of the police in relation to ministers might not have surfaced. Of course, policing never exists in a vacuum, isolated from political economy or social and cultural context: as Reiner argued the 'golden era' of policing in England and Wales coincided with a high level of political incorporation of working class interests, the development of the welfare state, and macro-economic policies that prioritised the maintenance of high levels of employment. As is argued later in the book, contemporary neoliberalism and globalisation create a political and economic landscape in which sustaining collective norms and values about the proper purposes of policing – prerequisites of accountability – are increasingly difficult.

While operational independence might be an important principle in regard to that very narrow definition of party politics, it is clear that policing, entailing as it does the deployment of state power, the denial of liberty (and even life) to some citizens and the capacity to intervene in private life, is inescapably political in more general terms (Police Foundation 2009; Reiner 2013). More widely still, while officers are prohibited from active party politics, they retain considerable power to shape public debate about matters of crime and social policy. Wall (1998) demonstrated that, historically, chief officers have been important players in local political elites, and Loader and Mulcahy (2001a, b) charted the 'soft power' that senior officers have exerted through contributing to policy debate across crime, social policy, health and other spheres. The police might be required to remain independent of party politics, but the central role that policing can play in the production and reproduction of social division, processes of 'social sorting' and the criminalisation of marginalised groups and activities means it is inherently political. The shared etymology of 'police' and 'politics', and that historically the term policing was used more widely to refer to the generic regulation of society, illustrates that policing is embedded in politics (Emsley 1996). Wood (2016) noted that liberal democratic conceptions have held that policing and the rule of law protect citizens from arbitrary state interference, but that the contemporary tendency to prioritise majoritarian populist approaches might mean police oppress minorities. The potential for 'democratic' but 'illiberal' policing, Wood (2016) argued, is increased in the wider environment of political populism and, conceivably, is a risk of having directly elected PCCs, a debate returned to in the next chapter.

As mentioned above, police are afforded greater legitimacy when held to account and so the connection to the 'golden thread' of democracy helps secure public support (Jarvis 2014). Hough et al's (2013) analysis of European public attitude data found that public trust in and compliance with police is closely related to perceptions of legitimacy. They suggest that the concept of police legitimacy comprises of trust in the police, belief that the rule of law applies, that they are effective and are accountable. This demonstrates the importance of accountability and oversight to the 'core business' of police maintaining order in society. It is possible to conceive of police forces in totalitarian regimes that are highly effective in deterring crime. However, since they operate with little oversight and are not accountable they are not considered legitimate and so can only secure compliance and cooperation through the threat of extreme negative repercussions, which is likely to be logistically as well as ethically untenable (although maybe effective in the short run). Conversely, Hough et al (2013) demonstrate that if the public perceive the police as fair and procedurally just, they will tend to regard them as legitimate (and that these were more significant perceptions than that the police were effective). In turn, high perceptions of legitimacy were associated with greater cooperation with police and stronger compliance with the law. As this and other studies demonstrate (Bradford 2014; Murphy et al 2014), operational and social benefits accrue from police accountability; these are not just abstract matters of moral preference or democratic theory. Procedural justice is also important internally in securing staff trust and confidence and support (Roberts and Herrington 2013). The need for police to recruit and retain a diverse workforce relates in part to securing wider public support, and so the promotion of organisational justice internally – which requires forms of accountability – is closely bound up with securing trust and confidence from the public at large (Workman-Stark 2017).

Policing beyond the nation state

Much of the discussion so far in this chapter has focused on the principles of accountability that have been applied to a model of policing developed over the last two centuries, usually associated with the establishment of the London Metropolitan Police in 1829. Rawlings (2005) argued that this event has 'transfixed' police historians, who have organised accounts of pre-1829 police history in teleological terms such that events are only seen as important insofar as they contributed to the establishment of the Met. Another consequence is that much of the writing about police and policing has tended to assume that this model is the natural order, and ideas about police accountability as sketched out in this chapter share this implicit assumption. In particular, the discussion has reflected the state-centric conception of policing: the organisation and delivery of state-authored law enforcement and service delivery administered in specific geographical units. From the organisational level of the constable's beat, through local command units, divisions and up to constabulary boundaries, policing tends to be organised geographically. Lustgarten (1986) perceptively tested arrangements for local accountability of police in England and Wales by considering the problems that mutual aid posed. He argued that such arrangements, designed to allow police to draw support from other forces around the country in times of crisis, were devised among networks of chief officers and backed by central government but were not subject to the oversight of local police authorities. These were controversial during the 1984–85 miners' strike, when police resources were coordinated nationally and officers deployed to frontline areas in ways that seemed to bypass local accountability and led many to argue that a de facto nationalised police service was operating under Home Office instructions. As is outlined in greater detail in several of the chapters that follow, similar problems of accountability apply writ large to policing in the 21st century. There are two, related, elements: first that policing increasingly operates across national borders, and second, that law enforcement activity increasingly tends to be delivered by agencies and organisations in the private sector.

Wider process of globalisation and technological developments in recent decades have meant that many public goods and services are 'disembedded' from nation state territories (Giddens 1999). Command and control approaches to public administration, governance and accountability become untenable in an era where law enforcement is delivered across national borders, let alone across the divisional boundaries of sub-national police services. Much of the development of cross-border policing follows growth in transnational crime and cross-border trade and commerce. Organised crime, terrorism, climate change and environmental degradation do not recognise state boundaries and require coordinated multinational responses. None of that is inherently problematic in terms of governance, but such developments do raise significant challenges since the 'hard' accountability mechanisms outlined in this book are predicated on the nation state as the central provider of oversight.

The 'hollowing out' of the state is not only a result of external pressures, but also a reflection of the decline of post-Second World War political, social and economic settlements and the rise of a neoliberal politics that has prioritised privatisation and monetarist economics, and has ceded power to global financial organisations (Sayer 2014). The consequences of this are profound for crime and policing as 'citizens' have become 'customers' and collective provisions of goods and services have been replaced by a rampant individualism that promotes 'private security' over public protection. Much more will be said about these developments in Chapter 8, the conclusion to this book. A more immediate implication is that the capacity of the state has been reduced. In relation to policing there has been a stark reduction in resources. In England and Wales, according to the Institute for Fiscal Studies, there was an overall reduction of 17.4 per cent in staff numbers from 2009 to 2016 and a 14 per cent decline in spending in real terms between 2010–11 and 2014–15 (Disney and Simpson 2017). The four dimensions of accountability cited from Jarvis (2014) earlier in the discussion each rely on state, government and bureaucracies, and some sense in which there is a public consensus about what constitutes a legitimate police service. Each of these core elements is problematic in a globalised neoliberal society. In response, the capacity of the state has shrunk in terms of delivering public services and the role has shifted to one of 'steering, not rowing', as Osborne and Gaebler (1992) incisively observed. In this model, the role of the state is to procure, coordinate and audit service delivery but not necessarily to provide those goods and services directly to the public. Into this new policing environment have stepped a range of community and third sector organisations, as well as private sector corporations, many of which are part of large global companies (Garland 2001). The apparent promise of 'predictive policing' poses further questions for those intent on retaining democratic control. Based on the notion that 'big data' policing and the development of powerful algorithms will allow the prediction of future offending and thus allow targeted early intervention, technological solutions offer the promise of more effective (and cost-effective) policing and a related reduction in the social harm caused by crime (Ferguson 2017). Disarmingly, part of the rhetorical appeal of such use of an evidence-based model of policing is that it appears to be a technocratic and value-free process that will establish the objective nature of crime risks. In practice, of course, the development of such data sets can never be a neutral or value-free exercise; the categorisation, compilation and processing of information relies on interpretation and judgement. In the context of crime mapping – an early form of what McLaughlin (2007) refers to as 'high definition' policing – Ratcliffe (2002) identified a series of issues that provide pause for ethical thought: the geographic information system (GIS) location of crime scenes was not always, he found, a simple or clear-cut process; the production of maps raised concerns about potential vigilantism and undermined the reputation of neighbourhoods already in straitened circumstances (as well as likely raising insurance premiums). In terms of the accountability of policing, the challenge becomes not how to hold to account the large IT and software companies who originate the algorithms that enable predictive policing, but, more problematically still, how those pieces of software are themselves governed in ways consistent with the wider interests of justice. Harcourt (2007) argues against such actuarial models of crime control on the basis that they distort understanding of offending patterns and through relentless criminalisation reduce ever further opportunities for 'lifestyle normalisation' and desistance.

Moreover, the extension of policing activities to include new agencies has entailed the incorporation of public- and private sector organisations that are not ostensibly or primarily involved in law enforcement. In the UK there are legal requirements for banks, communications and telecoms organisations and universities (for example) to report concerns about 'suspicious activity' (usually that which might be related to terrorism or organised crime, money laundering, and such like) to the relevant authorities, leading to what Mazerolle and Ransley (2005) termed 'third party' policing. This expansion from 'police' to 'policing' is further illustrated by the renaming in 2016 of the European Police College as the European Union Agency for Law Enforcement Training, as its remit expanded beyond police to incorporate agencies such as border patrols, fisheries and customs. Policing has also expanded as staff from other agencies within the criminal justice system, most obviously the probation service, have become subsumed with police in the practice of 'offender management', leading to the emergence of what Nash (1999) presciently dubbed the 'polibation officer'. Holding these forms of multi-agency policing networks to account is problematic using established 'hard' measures described above and in the next chapter, not least because the partner agencies themselves tend to be subject to their own mechanisms of accountability and governance.

In response to the increasingly diverse and fragmented policing environment, Loader and Walker (2007) advocated that security needs to be understood as a 'thick public good': a foundational requirement of social order necessary for collective and individual prosperity. In opposition to the notion of 'private security' – described by Stenson (2002) as an oxymoron since it prioritises individualism and undermines the potential for mutual reassurance – Loader and Walker (2007) advocate a model of 'anchored pluralism'. In this model, the state plays a central role in mediating public demands for security and provides resources and coordination for a 'civilised security', which entails (Loader and Walker 2007: 218–19):

> ... the state taking cognizance of the deep inequities in security provision generated by and through commercial security practices, and by the discrepancies in economic and social capital that afford individuals and groups such differential access to security capacity, and acting to deploy collective resources in order to bolster those constituencies who repeatedly lose, or do not even get to play, the market game.

A central benefit of this strategy is the reconciliation of the pluralisation and privatisation of security with the principles of collective provision necessary to secure democratic public interests. As the authors recognise, the challenge of securing anchored pluralism in relation to multi-layered transnational policing arrangements is significant, given its reliance on sovereign states. Not the least of the difficulties is the absence of coherent global norms and values required to underpin the development of a transnational model of democratic policing. Part of the problem is the absence of what Bowling and Sheptycki (2016) refer to as a 'global community' or *demos* that can articulate demand for democratic policing that promotes the rights of all. In practice, global policing arrangements sustain – rather than ameliorate – inequalities, and promote the interests of powerful elites at the expense of the Global South and marginalised populations (Fichtelberg 2015).

This chapter has introduced many themes that will be addressed and developed through the rest of the book and has provided some conceptual ground clearing for the discussion that follows. In some ways the principles and practices of accountability apply to police as to other public services but, it was argued, the symbolic status of the police as the 'state in uniform' with extensive powers over citizens means that effective governance is additionally important. Coupled with these powers is the inherent role of discretion in policing, and the low visibility of decisions that officers make. These, too, exacerbate the need for vigorous oversight mechanisms, and many of the policy and technological changes introduced around practices such as police stop and search and investigation of domestic abuse (to give just two examples) can be understood as techniques to increase the reach of police managers over the practice of operational staff. More on this follows in Chapter 6. Part of the challenge of reconciling officer discretion, which is inherent to policing, with the need for oversight and accountability is the problematic concept of operational independence. As has been outlined, the idea of operational independence – much cited in recent decades – has only shallow roots in the history of policing. In practical terms, operational independence quickly becomes problematic: officers might make their own decisions but they do not do so in circumstances of their own making, to paraphrase Karl Marx. The relatively recent development of strategies of EBP can be considered as a mechanism to regulate police discretion since it offers the potential for decision making to be exercised on the basis of robust scientific data. Officers will still be required to use their judgement (that is inherent to the role) but EBP is a form of professional practice that provides an opportunity for improved outcomes following scientific experimentation. As is discussed in much of what follows, this has implications for accountability. A debate is to be had between perceptions that increased professionalism and expert practice that can protect from the vagaries of populist demands on policing; alternatively EBP might be cast as anti-democratic in the sense that it removes policing from the legitimate demands of the public. An experiment conducted in 2015 by police in Leicestershire illustrated this tension. To test the value of dispatching scene of crime officers (SOCOs) to domestic burglary victims an experiment was developed such that some premises continued to get the service, while others did not. The early results suggested that there was little value in evidential terms in sending SOCOs to all burglary victims. While this appears to have been a sound experiment that enhanced the evidence base for policing, it was widely criticised by local and national politicians complaining of a 'postcode lottery' that denied some citizens a full police service. The conundrum is clear: on the one hand professional practice and on the other legitimate concerns that public trust and confidence in the legitimacy of police was undermined. Further discussion of EBP and accountability is developed in Chapter 5.

Developing effective accountability is problematic in contemporary societies in which policing is increasingly pluralised and networked across national boundaries. Private security, third-party policing and the 'securitisation' of swathes of public policy means that state-centred approaches to accountability, focusing predominantly or entirely on the public police service, need to be reconfigured. Not only does this mean bringing particular agencies or companies under the canopy of accountability frameworks, it requires regulation of the power inherent in complex networks of policing, and to do so on a transnational basis.

Note

[1]   *R v Commissioner of Police for the Metropolis, ex-parte Blackburn* [1968] 2 QB 118, CA, at 136.

Further reading

Edwards, A. (2016) 'Multi-centred Governance and Circuits of Power in Liberal Modes of Security'. *Global Crime*, 17(3–4): 240–63.

Jarvis, M.D. (2014) 'The Black Box of Bureaucracy: Interrogating Accountability in the Public Service', *Australian Journal of Public Administration*, 73(4): 450–66.

Mazerolle, L. and Ransley, J. (2005) *Third Party Policing*. Cambridge: Cambridge University Press.

3

Governance and politics of policing

Multi-level governance of policing incorporates a range of statutory mechanisms to hold police to account. Following on from the discussion of the principles of accountability in the previous chapter, in this section the focus moves on to analyse democratic policing in relation to its practical application across the four nations of the UK. The various roles of central government, PCCs, devolved and local government, and agencies such as Her Majesty's Inspectorate of Constabulary, Fire and Rescue Services (HMICFRS) will be critically analysed. It is argued that conventional approaches that distinguish between central and local sites of accountability are increasingly outmoded since the delivery of policing services transcends the borders of police constabulary areas. Moreover, the development of devolved government to the constituent nations within the UK means that national oversight is delivered in part at the sub-nation state level in UK terms. Furthermore, many of the national frameworks for accountability incorporate local actors, and vice versa. Since the national/local dichotomy is a useful heuristic model and reflects the historical development of police governance, it is retained in the structure of this chapter, which first analyses national and then local measures. As is shown, this is an artificial distinction in practice in an era in which policing is increasingly pluralised.

As the first two chapters have outlined, accountability is a multifaceted and multilayered set of practices. The discussion in this chapter focuses on the formal 'hard' mechanisms of accountability, the statutory and regulatory frameworks that are primarily concerned with the governance of public policing. The previous chapter outlined Romzek and Dubnick's (1987) four-way typology, which distinguished systems of accountability that offer either high or low levels of control, and are delivered either internally or externally. On this basis, most of the mechanisms reviewed in this chapter are intended to offer high levels of control delivered externally to the police by other public agencies. One of the key challenges for accountability of policing in the 21st century is that the established mechanisms reflect formalism following function as public police agencies have developed. As will be developed through the chapter, the pluralisation and transnationalism of contemporary policing reveal limitations, with formal mechanisms inevitably slow to respond to a fast-evolving policing landscape.

In the UK, police governance arrangements have developed as the organisation and delivery of police organisations has changed over time. Considering police governance and accountability in these terms reflects a 'formal-legal' approach (Lister and Jones 2016), suggesting mechanisms of accountability develop in the wake of changing functions of police agencies. Some of these arrangements are analysed below. While provisions have shifted, it is clear that there are considerable continuities spanning the period of almost two centuries since the 'new' Metropolitan Police were established in 1829. As noted in Chapter 2, this watershed date often misdirects historians of policing such that continuities between earlier systems of law enforcement and order maintenance and subsequent arrangements are overlooked (Rawlings 2005). With that in mind it is important to note that the separation of governance arrangements in the UK between local and central agencies, which has been a characteristic of the period since the mid nineteenth century when police forces were developed across the whole country, reflects much longer-standing provisions that can be traced back to the 12th century. The Police Act 1964 established the tripartite model of police governance, with powers separated between central government, local police authorities and chief constables who (as the previous chapter outlined) are deemed 'operationally independent'. As is outlined later in this chapter, the Police Reform and Social Responsibility Act 2011 replaced local police authorities with elected PCCs, who are themselves accountable to local Police and Crime Panels. While this has constituted a new 'quadripartite' system (Lister 2014), long-standing principles of local and central oversight remain. The chapter continues by critically reviewing the roles and responsibilities of central and local governance of policing in the UK. Chapter 8 considers the challenges of ensuring democratic governance and accountability in the transnational and global context, but it is argued below that some of the difficulties faced by cross-national borders reflect similar problems in terms of internal borders within the nation state, and between sectors and stakeholders. Furthermore, the increasing recognition and growth of plural policing also poses challenges of accountability and governance at the level of the nation state as well as transnationally.

Policing and the complexities of governance

Although the discussion that follows continues the tendency to consider police governance and accountability in spatial terms (delivered either nationally or locally), it is argued that the plethora of arrangements and practices charted here are complex and interdependent in ways that make this distinction misleading. The state-centric approach of much of the literature on democracy and policing is such that there has been a focus on powers and practices associated with particular government institutions. As Edwards (2016) indicated, established approaches to the analysis of state provision of security to citizens has relied on a model in which hierarchical power is the property of the executive and delegated down through tiers of subordinate layers of government. This 'command and control' model of government is increasingly untenable in a policing environment characterised by complex and interlocking provisions delivered collaboratively by various public sector agencies, civil society, private security and 'third party' organisations. The 'vertical chains of accountability that link providers of public services with institutional structures of the democratic polity' (Lister and Jones 2016: 193) are weakened or broken in the face of pluralised policing. This shift in conceptualisation of accountability mechanisms reflects a wider turn in approaches to the state and to government. Over recent decades, theorists of the state and political power have shifted focus from an organisational or institutional model to one that prefers instead to consider the exercise of power in terms of processes of 'governance'. Jessop (2016: 74) defined governance in terms that recognise that power is increasingly understood as decentralised, contested and relational: 'it refers to the diverse mechanisms and strategies of coordination that are adopted by autonomous actors, organizations and functional systems in the face of complex reciprocal interdependence among their actions, activities and operations'.

Edwards (2016) persuasively argued, in the particular context of the role of the state in the delivery of security, that recognition of governance as a form of networked activity should not be understood as the 'death of the state', since 'asymmetries' of power within these interdependent configurations of agencies remain. Fleming and Rhodes (2005) noted that shifts between 'bureaucratic', 'contract' and 'networked' models of police governance are overlapping and all three strategies can coexist simultaneously. The state retains a considerable, even pre-eminent, bureaucratic role within new assemblages of networked power, and in many jurisdictions the state has implemented 'contract' forms of governance through techniques of New Public Management. In this conceptualisation, and applied to the governance of policing, the state operates in a network of 'multi-centred power' in which it has a foundational role, but much contends with 'rival centres of power and resistance which aspirant governors, such as parents, teachers, municipal authorities, police forces and core executives, are obliged to negotiate' (Edwards 2016: 246). In relation to policing, this perspective is significant since it indicates that a hierarchical institutional model of police governance, such that the Home Office at the centre, and PCCs at the local level, are the primary offices that regulate police services, fails to capture the complexity of interlaced networks of overlapping systems of governance. Just as policing itself has become 'de-centred' in the sense that the delivery of law enforcement and social regulation is understood apart from the institution of police, so too governance is a process emerging from the interactions of a range of agencies. Conceiving of accountability in terms of governance is advantageous since it draws attention to the myriad and interdependent set of relationships through which a plethora of agencies – including central government, crown agencies, local politicians, civil society groups and 'non-departmental public bodies' – collectively provide for oversight. While this might be mutually provided in the sense that it emerges from the interaction of this network of actors, it should be recognised that there are tensions and contradictions in governance of policing. Against this background, Loader and Walker (2007) have argued that democratic governance of the 'public good' of policing can be retained, even in a pluralised environment, by developing a model of 'anchored pluralism' (as introduced in the previous chapter). They argued that interconnected policing and security services, delivered by myriad national, local, public, private and third-party agencies, can be 'civilised' by the state, which would retain the foundational role in processing public demand and providing resources.

Some elements within the governance arrangements for police are primary actors in the sense that their remit is primarily and formally to hold police services or staff to account in some aspect. These are the structures delivering high levels of external control in Romzek and Dubnick's (1987) model. As established in 1856, HMIC is a primary agent of police government, although the Policing and Crime Act 2017 recast the organisation as HMICFRS. This extension in the mandate reflected wider pressures on police and other emergency services to work collaboratively, and some PCCs have assumed oversight of local fire services. Given the expansion of police roles through engagement with partner agencies, extending the remit of oversight agencies may be a logical institutional development, although many stakeholders expressed concern that this would intensify competition for resources between the services. Furthermore, the incorporation of police services with other emergency responders casts the police mandate in responsive law enforcement terms. The considerable resources that police expend working with other agencies in the social, health and education sectors – and the increasing emphasis that police in England and Wales place on their role in protecting vulnerable citizens – is, at least symbolically, marginalised by governance arrangements that position police services with fire and rescue responders. The extension of the role of PCCs further embeds their engagement with local government, since local councillors form the Fire and Rescue Authority that oversees each county's service.

National accountability and governance

The pre-eminent central government oversight of policing has emanated from the Home Office. Not only did the Home Secretary act as the local police authority for the Metropolitan Police (before the Police Reform and Social Responsibility Act 2011 transferred this duty to the Mayor) but the Home Office provides funding to the other 42 'home' police services in England and Wales, supplemented with funds raised by the local policing levy set by PCCs. In terms of regulating police priorities and practices, the Home Office produces national policing plans, 'strategic policing requirements' and a plethora of 'circulars' with which local police services must comply. Within the Home Office a range of boards and units provide detailed advice and support to influence policing policy. Many of these – such as the Police Advisory Board (which addresses matters relating to police pension arrangements) – comprise stakeholders that have their own distinct roles within police accountability. That the National Police Chiefs' Council (representing senior officers, and discussed further in Chapter 6) and the Association of Police Crime Commissioners (APCC; discussed in relation to local accountability later in this chapter) are represented on this board further demonstrates the interlocking nature of central and local mechanisms and that operational police are also engaged, illustrating further the complexity of governance arrangements.

A key mechanism underpinning Home Office oversight of police is the annual inspection carried out by HMICFRS to assess the extent to which constabularies meet the criteria of 'effectiveness, efficiency and legitimacy'. While many of the questions that underpin these assessments are couched in local terms (including, for example, 'how effectively does the force understand the communities it serves?'), they also consider the extent to which national standards and priorities are met. On the basis of these reviews, forces are graded as 'outstanding', 'good', 'requires improvement' or 'inadequate', and are required to produce plans to address issues of concern. In 2005 the Home Office

Police Standards Unit seconded senior staff from West Midlands Police into Nottinghamshire police following an inspection that found the latter was under-performing in tackling serious crime. For such reasons Loveday (2005: 275) referred to the increasing power of central government relative to local agencies, noting the 'central determination of ostensibly local policing'. The HMICFRS inspections are explicitly based on a consumer model, casting accountability and governance in terms of a model predicated on public feedback and 'consumer "watchdog" tactics, such as mystery shopping' (as outlined on the HMICFRS website). While these are not the only methods used to identify police efficiency, effectiveness and legitimacy, they provide a form of accountability with limited scope to consider structural or institutional concerns about the impact of policing on marginalised, disadvantaged and socially excluded populations. As is discussed in relation to PCCs the risk of majoritarian authoritarianism remains in this model, such that the mainstream of public perceptions might be favourable, but rights and status of minority groups neglected. Similar concerns arise in relation to the occasional role of the National Audit Office in police governance, providing, as it does, a managerialist financial review of police (and other) services to establish that value for money is secured. The reform and restructuring of police services instigated to achieve such outcomes might be in tension with local mechanisms for accountability. Recent financial constraints, for example, have led to some police services pooling 'back office' management and support services (such as helicopter air support, for example) and to the privatisation of some facilities previously provided in house. These might be appropriate responses in managerial and technical terms but the development of cross-service provisions of this kind removes control, to an extent, from local oversight. Challenges for accountability that arise in transnational policing, analysed in Chapter 8, apply more locally in terms of cross-force collaboration (Lustgarten 1986).

The National Crime Agency (NCA), responsible for serious crime, terrorism, economic crime and human trafficking – threats deemed to transcend local police services – is accountable directly to the Home Office, and to the Scottish Parliament and the Northern Ireland Assembly. In common with local police services, the NCA is subject to inspection by HMICFRS and the National Audit Office, and staff are subject to the oversight of the IOPC. That the NCA is an important node within contemporary networked policing demonstrates that mechanisms for local accountability lack capacity in certain key respects. In this specific context, while the

NCA operates nationally and internationally, it engages in routine operational policing with local police services. This reflects that for all the focus on transnational patterns of organised crime, ultimately all crime is experienced locally, by particular people in specific locations. In law the Director General of the NCA can instruct chief constables to engage in 'tasking and assistance arrangements', should voluntary agreement not be forthcoming. The scope for PCCs to exercise oversight of such mutual assistance is limited and, in times of constrained resources, the capacity of police services to respond to local demand curtailed if officers and staff are 'abstracted' to work with the NCA. While this might not be problematic in legal or normative terms, it does illustrate a further fuzzy boundary between local and national direction of police.

Other central agencies engaged in police governance can be considered secondary, either in the sense that their oversight of policing is only one component of a wider mandate, or that they address only a de-limited aspect of policing activity. In the latter category is the Office of Surveillance Commissioners (OSC), responsible for ensuring that undercover surveillance by police is necessary, proportionate and consistent with civil liberties and privacy law. The OSC provider oversight on similar terms for intelligence services, prisons, local government and other regulatory agencies. The OSC's work has become particularly important in response to recognition that 'spy police' have operated in England and Wales since the late 1960s to monitor groups engaged in lawful political protest and campaigns (Evans and Lewis 2013). Media reports that police taskforces such as the Special Demonstrations Squad (whose unofficial motto was 'by any means necessary': Hadjimatheou [2017: 279]) and the National Public Order Intelligence Unit had infiltrated political and social campaign groups, had developed personal and sexual relationships with those involved, and were alleged to have committed criminal acts, led, in 2015, to the establishment of the Pritchard Inquiry to review, among other things, the management and oversight of such work. Revelations of the police role in monitoring 'subversive' groups are of particular concern since they invoke not only questions of civil liberties, but also of privacy, state power and the exercise of fundamental democratic political rights (Lubbers 2015). Although political policing in this form has a long history (Bunyan 1977) – and is a central component of 'high policing' intended to protect the state (Brodeur 1983) – it is clearly in tension with the model of liberal democratic policing outlined by Wood (2016), which is predicated on the role of police in protecting citizens from state encroachment on fundamental human rights.

Local accountability and governance

Conceptually, analysis of the governance of policing in Britain has presented local mechanisms as counterweights to the national frameworks sketched above. The much-mythologised 'genius' of the modern police established in 1829 is held in large part to have been the reconciliation of an enhanced role for the central nation state with historical traditions of local control. Through protecting the local roots of policing, orthodox histories contend, the potential for police to become tyrannical agents of central government was averted (Reiner 2010). Nonetheless, as was briefly noted in Chapter 2, the subordinate status of local oversight relative to central direction and control is evident and has been a cause for concern for many decades. Coupled with the extension of community safety partnerships that have incorporated local authorities, third-party and private security services into local policing networks (which have been outside the remit of local police accountability mechanisms), the decline in local democratic oversight of police has been widely lamented. The demise of local accountability has been a long-standing theme in police scholarship. One of the earliest books exploring police government in England and Wales (Marshall 1965: 46) observed that 'local accountability has been hindered and its operation rendered uncertain both by the supposed legal status of constables and by the existence of the Home Secretary's statutory powers'. More recently, in the wake of the development of national arrangements implemented during the 1984–85 miners' strike (outlined in Chapter 2), Reiner (1992: 29) argued that 'local accountability has been eroded'.

It was in this context that the directly elected PCCs were introduced in England and Wales to replace the local police authorities (comprised of local councillors, magistrates and independent appointments) set up by the Police Act 1964. The PCC system was proposed as a response to concerns that police authorities lacked visibility, and so legitimacy, among the public and that their replacement with a directly elected Commissioner would increase scrutiny of local police (Loveday 2013). The White Paper prefiguring the legislation also couched the new role in the wider terms of the Coalition Government's 'localism agenda', such that power over policing would be 'moved out of Whitehall' and returned 'to Chief Constables, their staff and the communities they serve' (Home Office 2010: 2, cited in Lister and Rowe 2015: 359). To avoid concerns that granting a single individual extensive control over police resourcing and the appointment of senior officers (among the other roles of PCCs) might prove problematic, Police and Crime Panels (PCPs) were established to hold PCCs to account (becoming the 'fourth leg' of the new quadripartite settlement).

The democratic credentials of the new office were undermined by a very low level of public engagement in the first round of elections in 2012, at which turnout was – by some distance – the lowest recorded in any national election in England and Wales (Lister and Rowe 2015). Caless and Owens' (2016) interviews with PCCs found that the weakness of their electoral mandate was invoked by some chief police officers who sought to challenge the scope and power of their new local overseers. While the second round of PCC elections in 2016 saw an increase in turnout that reduced this deficit, other concerns about the democratic legitimacy of the PCC system are inherent. Among these are the vexed problem of representation, since PCCs are expected to represent local priorities but still on a relatively large scale compared to other elected roles. The PCC for a metropolitan force would typically be expected to 'represent' a population of two or three million people across 30 parliamentary constituencies, and yet research evidence suggests that concerns about crime, antisocial behaviour and policing can be incoherent and contradictory even at much smaller neighbourhood levels (Hughes and Rowe 2007). Another inherent concern is the risk of majoritarian populism since, in electoral terms, PCCs are likely not to have to court the needs of marginalised or minority groups. As Reiner (2016: 139) has argued, the PCC model equates democratic credibility entirely with elections, which are a 'necessary but not sufficient condition of democracy' and need to be coupled with civil, social and economic rights if democratic citizenship is to flourish. The majoritarian imperative means not only that the concerns about over-policing or the abuse of power are unlikely to be addressed by police, but that 'difficult' topics might be avoided altogether in local debate. The involvement of directly elected PCCs in police accountability has the potential to heighten the tension between liberal values and democracy (Wood 2016). In an environment where PCCs represent large and diverse populations, the need to secure a majority at the ballot box might mean that the rights of minority groups are sidelined or even compromised (Lister and Rowe 2015): thus might emerge a PCC with democratic credentials in electoral terms but not in relation to the civil and social economic components of citizenship outlined by Marshall (1950, cited in Reiner, 2016). The electoral priorities of candidates seeking to become a PCC might explain the focus on a narrow range of conventional law and order themes evident in the manifestos produced in the first set of elections

(Lister and Rowe 2016). Similarly, Wells' (2016) analysis showed that the issue of roads policing, if addressed at all by PCCs in their election campaign materials, was couched in terms consistent with dominant narratives about joy-riding, uninsured and untaxed drivers and links to serious and organised criminal activity. Offences (and the related harm, injury and death) that might be caused by the majority of 'respectable' drivers did not figure in PCC campaigns. Indeed Wells (2016) cited a case where a PCC publicly declared that fines should not be levied on 'ordinary motorists' since to do so would reduce public support for police: a pledge that impinges on the principle of operational independence.

Constitutionally, the work of PCCs is overseen by the local PCPs, although the emerging record is chequered and ambiguous – to some degree because PCCs are required to consult the Panels on some matters but are not subservient to them. Chambers' (2014) analysis of the first year of the PCC system found that PCPs rarely challenged decisions made by PCCs, although some national agencies (the Parliamentary Home Affairs Select Committee and the Welsh Assembly) provided more critical review of the role of PCCs. This further demonstrates the intertwined nature of national and local mechanisms of accountability. A similar theme emerges from analysis of some of the more high-profile incidents involving PCC relations with chief officers, given that PCCs have the power to require senior police to resign. Section 38 of the 2011 Act stipulates that these powers can be invoked by the PCC on the grounds of 'effectiveness and efficiency' but only after consultation with the local PCP and with Her Majesty's Chief Inspector. The extent and nature of this power was questioned in the cases where the Chief Constable of Avon and Somerset was 'required to resign' following allegations of misconduct (which do not necessarily constitute matters of 'effectiveness and efficiency' [Hales 2015]) and the case of the Chief Constable of South Yorkshire, in which the High Court ruled in 2017 that the PCC had not adequately consulted the local PCP and the national HMI. Safeguards against the arbitrary or inappropriate removal of senior officers further illustrates the mutuality of local and national accountability measures. The development of a corporate national body – the APCC – was intended, among other things, to facilitate PCC 'leadership on national governance structures' of the kind outlined earlier in this chapter. While the provision of support for individual PCCs might strengthen their capacity to engage in governance arrangements relative to national agencies that have considerable legal, cultural and organisational capital at hand, other aspects of this element of the APCC's work raises questions in terms of independence and governance. A high-profile example is outlined in the APCC's 2017 annual report, which includes details of the development of the *Policing Vision 2025* with the National Police Chiefs' Council (whose role is discussed in Chapter 6). Co-production and collaboration of this type raises important questions about the extent to which PCCs are subject to bureaucratic 'capture' by the agencies that they are supposed to hold to account.

National policing in Scotland

In Scotland, formal local accountability disappeared when eight forces, overseen in part by local government, were merged into a single national service – Police Scotland – accountable directly to the Scottish Government under the auspices of the Scottish Police Authority (SPA). Members are appointed to the SPA by ministers, who have oversight and funding responsibilities similar to those in other jurisdictions and must produce an annual report, and other performance reviews, and financial auditing on behalf of the Scottish Parliament. Unlike in England and Wales, the SPA is also responsible for the provision of forensic services to Police Scotland, on the basis that independence of those from the Chief Constable will protect the integrity of the evidence delivered. Commentators have argued that the profile of police in Scotland has risen following the unification of the Service and that some of the early problems of accountability could be attributed to a lack of clarity around new roles and divisions of responsibilities (Scott 2015). Certainly, some of the difficulties – particularly in relation to the status of local accountability – seem to stem directly from the legislative framework (the Police and Fire Reform (Scotland) Act 2012) that made Police Scotland itself responsible for developing local engagement and accountability (Flanagan 2016). As was argued in relation to police in England and Wales in the 1980s and 1990s, these arrangements confuse consultation with accountability since the terms on which engagement occurs remain in the hands of the police (Keith 1988). Moreover, marginalised groups that are relatively powerless compared to police are unlikely to effectively engage at the local level: after all, these might be the groups for whom the police are the problem, and not a viable agency to bring about reform (McLaughlin 1991). A review of police governance (Flanagan 2016) followed a series of controversies about, among other things, stop and search practices and the use of force, and reflected a fundamental clash in terms of the principles of police accountability outlined in Chapter 2. Scott (2015) argued that the various scandals encircling Police Scotland in the first years of its existence stem from the difficulties of reconciling political oversight with operational independence.

Police reform and community engagement in Northern Ireland

Not surprisingly, similar challenges apply in many models of police accountability. That introduced in Northern Ireland has developed alongside the wider peace process of the last decades, and the creation of the Police Service of Northern Ireland (PSNI) (replacing the Royal Ulster Constabulary and consciously seeking a post-sectarian identity) has been a key element of power sharing and devolved government (Independent Commission on Policing for Northern Ireland 1999). In Northern Ireland, as in other post-conflict societies, police reform has been an important component of wider political and social transition. Ellison (2007) noted that for all that arrangements for accountability represented a blueprint for other countries, he also identified that some of the limitations evident have arisen from constraints in the wider political and civil sectors. His point is further illustrated since, for a lengthy period from 2017 onwards, the Northern Ireland Assembly has been suspended and so the governance of policing has reverted, along with other matters, to the UK government in Westminster. Otherwise arrangements continue under the auspices of the Northern Ireland Policing Board (NIPB), which differs somewhat from the Scottish model since it does not process complaints against police nor provide forensic services. Topping (2016) noted that the NIPB had a broader remit than many of the other oversight agencies in the UK. The Independent Commission on Policing for Northern Ireland (1999) set the parameters of the NIPB to govern police but also to extend more widely to include the contributions made by other agencies to the delivery of public safety (Topping 2016: 155). In practice, however, the global 'gold standard' for police accountability that the Northern Ireland model had been held to represent has been constrained in the face of 'mediating realities', including the continuing threat of terrorism, social and religious divisions and alternative forms of policing.

Local accountability is embedded in the Northern Ireland model through community safety partnerships to which district councils are required to appoint councillors in proportion to local electoral outcomes. The partnerships also include independent members, also nominated by district councils, and again these need to broadly represent the local community. The role of the partnerships is to facilitate public engagement and consultation, to question and monitor police activity and to contribute to the wider promotion of community safety in their areas. Quite what resources or powers members of the partnerships have to deliver these broad and complex outcomes is unclear but, in formal terms at least, the Northern Ireland model is multi-layered and inclusive. One of the wider challenges relating to police accountability outlined at various stages in this text is that there is an underlying need for a degree of normative consensus relating to what the outcomes of legitimate policing might be. In high-conflict or post-conflict societies, including Northern Ireland, the lack of such commonality demonstrates that formal arrangements for 'hard' accountability are necessary but insufficient conditions for effective governance. As Ellison (2007: 244) identified, achieving democratic oversight of the PSNI is a significant challenge given that one of the largest parties in the province did not recognise the legitimacy of the police service until 2007.

Networked policing, accountability and governance

Recent decades have seen increasing recognition of the role of non-public police agencies in the delivery of policing, security management and regulation (Shearing and Stenning 1981). While some have argued that this emerging focus on private policing, or plural policing as it is more often referred to, tends to elide the lengthy history of co-production of such services (Jones and Newburn 1998) it is clear that only recently have the implications of networks of multiple policing providers for democratic accountability been considered (Johnston and Shearing 2003). The lack of mechanisms in many western liberal democracies to effectively regulate private security as a public good subject to democratic control is widely noted, as will be outlined in the discussion that follows. Moreover, it is argued that the broader social, political and economic trends that have occasioned the growth of pluralised policing have also undermined the capacity of the state and civil society to provide for effective oversight.

The emergence of plural policing in recent decades is usually explained in terms of wider structural changes in western societies such that the inherent capacity of the state to provide public goods has declined as a result of a retreat from mid 20th-century welfarism and interventionist economic policy (Johnston 1992). McLaughlin (2007) argued that the state has been 'de-centred' from the provision of policing, opening up increasing space for private sector engagement. Coupled with economic and bureaucratic limitations on the capacity of the state to deliver provisions directly to the public has been the development of neoliberal ideology that prioritises a smaller role for the state. The subsequent withdrawal of public provisions across a whole raft of policy areas has been to the benefit of private providers who have filled the vacuum. Although, in Britain, this shift has been less pronounced, and later in arriving, in the context of policing (relative to health or transport, for example) the lack of capacity of the state to meet emerging demands for policing and security is increasingly apparent.

Bound up with the contraction of the state and the expansion of private security has been the process of 'responsibilisation', such that public agencies and private corporations not primarily engaged in law enforcement or security have been conjoined with police and other regulators in activities intended to tackle organised crime, terrorism, and immigration control, for example. The concept of responsibilisation is usefully applied to the developments in multi-agency provision of community safety that followed in the wake of the Crime and Disorder Act (CDA) 1998, which created a legal duty for local government to promote crime prevention and measures to tackle antisocial behaviour (Burney 2009). It is this process that has created 'third party' policing (Mazerolle and Ransley 2005) such as that practised in the financial sector, required by the Terrorism Act 2000 and the Proceeds of Crime Act 2002, to report to any activity among clients that might be connected to criminal activity to the NCA. Similarly, universities are required to monitor student attendance and behaviour as a check against abuse of student visas, fraudulent applications for student finance, and to counter radicalisation (the 'prevent duty' established by the Counter Terrorism and Security Act 2015). Garland (2001) showed that processes of responsibilisation has extended to private citizens. Among the provisions of the CDA 1998 were 'parenting orders' directed at those with children causing antisocial behaviour, and requirements for private landlords to monitor their tenants, and in more generic terms the encouragement of citizens to assume responsibility for the security of their persons and property. Private companies offering apparent technological solutions to such threats have escalated citizen demand for security and nurtured markets through escalating public perceptions of risk and threat (Lee 2007; Lee and Farrall 2009). Counter-intuitively, the expansion of private solutions to insecurity and anxiety has driven the very concerns they ostensibly promised to allay. Similarly, provisions of additional street patrols in response to heightened public demand have been found ineffective since they too served to escalate expectations further than could be met, even by enhanced levels of service (Crawford and Lister 2006).

Related to this is the 'mass private property' thesis, which identifies the increasing tendency for routine activities (once located in civic and public arenas) to be conducted in private spaces. The shift in retail and leisure activities to private malls often is identified as representing a wider shift in social life to geographical spaces that are regulated by private security agencies; territories over which the public police have looser powers and control (Kempa et al 2004). Coleman (2005) showed how the reconfiguration of public space affects perceptions and practices of moral order, security and regulation and incorporates new assemblages of public, private and third-party policing networks that develop technologies of surveillance that utilise data and software developed in the private sector. The resultant practices of regulation have a material impact on access to urban space, and behaviours that are 'tolerated' within them, establishing what Millie (2008) described as an 'urban aesthetic' that identifies forms of antisocial behaviour not to be tolerated in these environments.

The social, economic and political processes – only briefly sketched above – are significant to debates about democratic governance since they explain the depth and complexity of networked policing as it develops in late modern society. The lattice of policing and security provision is such that the hierarchical approach to government, with implicit models of power relations emanating from a core central executive, that have dominated approaches to police accountability are increasingly untenable. Governance, referring back to Jessop's definition, needs instead to be understood as a process; it is contested, relational and in flux. Arrangements are in place for regulating particular institutions within these networks (as outlined above), and offices such as the Security Industry Authority have developed in the UK in recognition that previously neglected (by accountability mechanisms) policing agencies are becoming increasingly significant. However, as theorists of networked governance note, the relational nature of power within networks is not subject to effective regulation when the systems to deliver that are focused on individual nodal points among complex webs (Wood and Shearing 2007). It is for these reasons that Lister and Jones (2016: 207) argued that

> … there is no oversight mechanism for the totality of 'nodal policing' in any given locale. This is not to argue that plural policing networks are completely unaccountable and unregulated: elements of such networks clearly do operate with varying degrees of accountability to different audiences. It remains the case, however, that under current

institutional arrangements in England and Wales there
are no formal mechanisms for rendering plural policing
networks as a whole accountable to democratic values.

Chapters that follow will outline various mechanisms – formal and
informal, hard and soft, internal and external – that regulate aspects
of plural policing networks. Furthermore, reports of the 'death of
the state' are greatly exaggerated and it is clear that – while the state's
capacity to govern along the lines of a hierarchical Hobbesian Leviathan
might no longer be taken for granted and is checked by competing
sources of power domestically and internationally – governments
and public bureaucracies continue to exercise considerable financial,
political, legal and cultural power. On this basis, Loader and Walker
(2007) called for 'anchored pluralism', as noted in the introduction
to this chapter, such that the state occupied a foundational role in
guaranteeing that normative standards are applied to policing and
ensuring that fundamental human rights and equity apply in a
pluralised policing environment.

   As is discussed at various points in the remainder of this book, and
in Chapter 8 in particular, pluralised policing is significant in terms of
democratic accountability and governance in ways that extend beyond
the important legal and logistical challenge of overseeing complex
multi-layered policing systems. The socio-political changes that have
created the circumstances in which new forms of policing provisions
have thrived also serve to undermine the basis for collective debate
and the establishment of normative standards around which coherent
democratic demands for police services can be articulated. The network
of pluralised providers of policing is not only problematic in terms of
democratic accountability because of its fragmented, fluid and complex
nature, it also – in the absence of effective oversight – contributes to
the erosion of the social and civic bonds that are central to enabling
conditions of democratic governance. Following Bauman's (2000, cited
in Gadd and Jefferson 2009) argument, the development of the neoliberal
individualism that helped to occasion the growth of plural policing has
given rise to a trade-off between common security and individual free
choice and consumption. One outcome of this has been that ontological
security has been replaced by mutual suspicion and widespread anxiety.

Conclusion

The discussion above illustrates that the conventional distinction
between national and local sites of police governance in the UK

is untenable in the face of networks of policing that transcend organisational constabulary boundaries and incorporate multiple public, private and third-party agencies. As has been shown, many have noted that national government mechanisms, largely emanating from the Home Office, have had significantly greater power than other parties within tripartite arrangements from the 19th to the early 21st century, and that this continues in the quadripartite model established by the Police Reform and Social Responsibility Act 2011. The need to move beyond a national/local conceptualisation of police governance is made more pressing by other developments, beyond the imbalance of power within that framework. As the overview in this chapter indicates, the intertwined roles of nominally national and local agencies are considerable. National bodies such as HMICFRS have a formal duty in relation to local PCC powers to hold chief officers to account. Conversely, through their professional association, local PCCs are embedded in the development of policy and strategy at the national level. None of this is necessarily legally or normatively problematic but these developments highlight that a national/local understanding of police governance obscures contemporary practice. It has also been shown, in various contexts, that wider constitutional changes within the UK state have introduced new layers within the multiple sites of police governance. Devolution of policing powers, to different extents, to the Scottish Parliament, the Welsh Assembly, and the Northern Ireland Assembly have created new planes of national accountability at the sub-state level in UK terms.

Shifting and dissolving boundaries surrounding the delivery of policing in more general terms also mean that the framework of constabularies, each with local and national oversight, needs to be recast. The pluralisation of policing has meant that agencies and partners not held to account by the mechanisms applied to the public police are increasingly embroiled in the delivery of law enforcement and community safety. Local government, private security and third-party agencies are themselves subject to governance and oversight regimes but are not captured by the governance of the police. More fundamentally, the 'formal-legal' approach to accountability (Lister and Jones 2016) focuses on institutional oversight and not the networks of power that emerge from the interaction and co-delivery of policing services across complex lattices of diverse agencies. The impact that networked policing has in terms of power over citizens – which Chapter 2 identified as the core reason why democratic accountability is imperative – is considerable but nebulous and elusive since it is not retained within the auspices of discrete bounded institutions. This chapter has also introduced arguments that will be developed further throughout the book to the effect that the underlying economic, social and political transformations that have created the space for pluralised policing are bound up with individualism, responsibilisation and a decline in civic engagement, which erode the basis for the development of the public good of policing services. This is the core argument developed in Chapter 8.

Further reading

Lister, S. and Rowe, M. (eds) (2016) *Accountability of Policing*. London: Routledge.

Loader, I. and Walker, N. (2007) *Civilising Security*. Cambridge: Cambridge University Press.

Wood, D.A. (2016) 'The Importance of Liberal Values within Policing: Police and Crime Commissioners, Police Independence and the Spectre of Illiberal Democracy', *Policing and Society*, 26: 148–64.

4

Complaints and discipline

Whereas the focus of the previous chapter was on those mechanisms of governance and accountability that provide oversight and direction in broad terms, the discussion below considers the systems for responding to complaints relating to misconduct or malfeasance at the level of individual police officers or particular operational activities. Returning to the distinction between accountability as a set of practices providing for future governance and accountability as a retrospective process to review past performance, systems for investigating alleged wrongdoing have tended to be in the latter category. It is argued later in the chapter that the key development in England and Wales has been to increase transparency in the investigation of complaints against police, although the benefits of this might not be as significant in and of themselves. In terms of Jarvis's (2014) typology of accountability, the investigation of complaints against police connects most clearly to democratic principles since they respond to potential abuse of state power and the maintenance of trust and legitimacy. As is outlined further below, in the UK there has been a more recent development of strategies to promote opportunities for organisational learning (another of Jarvis's categories) presented by the effective investigation of complaints.

A combination of civil and criminal legal routes provide formal mechanisms for remedies and restitutions following police misconduct, as is reviewed in this chapter. These can be considered as systems of accountability that offer high levels of external control, as delineated in Romzek and Dubnick's (1987) typology of systems of accountability. Impressionistically, at least, it seems that the adequacy of these provisions is questioned in many liberal democratic societies. As is outlined below, concerns about the conduct of investigations into complaints against police have tended to coalesce around arguments that these are insufficiently robust and are not independent of police services under investigation. In the UK context the contemporary history of police complaints systems has been characterised by successive efforts to boost their independence, but such developments continue to face challenges relating to the inherent nature of police discretion, occupational culture and dimensions of police work itself, all of which are cited as significant, perhaps insurmountable, obstacles to transparency. Other changes to police complaints processes are also reviewed, including the development of early warning indicators, mediation and informal methods of resolution. All of these represent ways of improving effectiveness and public and police support for systems to respond to complaints, which have been widely regarded as failing in many countries. Prenzler and Porter (2016: 65) identified elements of emerging good practice that might turn around the very unsatisfactory position they characterised in the following terms:

> In traditional police complaints systems, large numbers of allegations are made by dissatisfied citizens and processed by police in an adversarial system ostensibly concerned with fact-finding and due process. Very few complaints are substantiated and there is a wide-ranging view that the system is biased against complainants and fails to provide proper democratic accountability for the exercise of police powers. Nothing much changes.

The challenge of investigating police misdemeanours

There are a number of reasons, as Prenzler and Porter (2016) outlined, why the task of investigating police complaints is inherently challenging. First, the diverse nature of claims made against police means that a wide range of processes and outcomes is required. While a significant proportion of complaints relate to allegations of incivility in police encounters with the public and might be appropriately addressed by relatively straightforward 'local resolution', such as an apology, others concern more serious matters, including deaths in custody or corruption, and so have the potential for criminal charges. Second, the nature of police work itself – and the very reason why accountability is crucial to public legitimacy – is such that complaints might be made for vexatious reasons by individuals seeking to discredit police actions. Indeed, there are mechanisms within the complaints system in England and Wales to dismiss complaints judged to be made for such reasons. The need to protect the position of police staff from unwarranted accusations, while giving proper attention to legitimate matters of public concern and the interests of individual complainants is a difficult task. Ensuring that the former interests are properly recognised lies behind the tendency for complaints to be investigated within quasi-legal disciplinary frameworks, with the rights of those subject to complaint formally represented by police unions and legal advisors. The disciplinary-based approach to responding to police complaints has been understood as counter-productive to efforts to develop early warning indicators that might identify potentially problematic behaviour, or to use complaints as opportunities for wider organisational learning (approaches that are held to have been developed more successfully in other sectors and organisations (Shane 2013)).

Furthermore, the nature of police work and the exercise of police discretion mean that actions that might lead to complaints are often carried out in conditions of 'low visibility', beyond not only the oversight of managers, but also isolated from public bystanders or witnesses (Rowe 2007). In such conditions, establishing the veracity of competing accounts of an encounter is particularly difficult. Efforts to overcome this limitation through the use of CCTV systems in police premises, the use of Body Worn Cameras (BWCs) and the increasing use of informal public surveillance delivered via camera phone and social media can be considered as potential means of increasing transparency. These and related developments, both internal and external to police services, are considered further in Chapters 6 and 7.

Having outlined developing arrangements to investigate complaints against the public police service, the chapter will review limitations of formal mechanisms by considering the scope of civil litigation in England and Wales to seek restitution following alleged wrongdoing, and the associated advantages and disadvantages such actions offer relative to other routes.

Police complaints in England and Wales

Until the mid 1970s, the police in England and Wales were responsible for recording and responding to complaints made against their officers in a model that had no semblance of independence. The establishment of the Police Complaints Board in 1976 did not significantly alter this, although the introduction of a national body to provide oversight of trends and patterns increased focus on tackling emerging concerns about police corruption and racism. Further, the Board had the capacity to ensure that more serious allegations were investigated by officers from another force, and the creation of this minimal distance between investigator and the subject of investigation shows that concerns about bias were prevalent. Since that period, other reforms have incrementally increased the degree of independence in complaints systems, although this remains partial rather than absolute. While formal independence now operates in England and Wales in the sense that more serious allegations of misconduct are directly investigated by staff of the Independent Office for Police Conduct, it continues to be the case that the vast majority of claims are investigated by Professional Standards Departments (PSDs) internal to police services. In 2016–17, police services recorded 34,103 complaints, and the Independent Police Complaints Commission (IPCC) (the forerunner to the IOPC) instigated 590 investigations (IPCC 2017, 2018). That the overwhelming majority of complaints against police continue to be recorded and investigated by the police service about which the complaint is made might be legitimate in terms of processing 'low-level' matters, providing a timely response and providing for learning opportunities at the local level, but it indicates that the independence of investigations continues to be limited. A lack of independent investigation notwithstanding, there continue to be high levels of general public confidence in the complaints system. The 2016 IPCC survey on public confidence found that 62 per cent were 'very' or 'fairly' confident that complaints are treated fairly (Ipsos MORI 2016). In contrast, however, are lower levels of satisfaction among those who have actually made a complaint to police. Research interviews carried out on behalf of the IPCC with 25 people who had been through local resolution processes in response to low-level complaints found that ten were 'very dissatisfied' with the investigating officer (Hearnden and May 2013). Further, 14 reported that they were 'not confident at all' in the handling of their case and that this was often related to a perceived lack of independence in the investigation. As Torrible (2016) argued, these contrasting findings indicate a fundamental problem in assessing the effectiveness of complaints systems: if public confidence is the key benchmark then it appears a successful system operates, but if providing restitution to individual complaints is regarded as more significant then more negative conclusions are to be drawn.

IOPC powers were extended in 2019 to include the ability to proactively launch investigations where cases are not referred by a police service and a new legal duty on officers to 'cooperate fully' with investigations. Although both appear to be incremental changes, they reflect wider concerns relating to the central role police services continue to play in the investigation of complaints. The extent to which the IOPC will launch its own investigations remains to be seen; clearly its capacity in this regard will be determined to a significant extent by the resources provided to the agency. In the case of its predecessor, the IPCC, the ability to fulfil the 'guardianship role' of investigating matters of policy and organisational practice that give rise to public concern was limited as resources were directed at responding to individual cases. A report of Parliament's Home Affairs Committee (2013b) described IPCC resources as 'woefully inadequate', even in terms of providing proper responses to individual allegations of wrongdoing, let alone wider matters of policy. If properly resourced, the new powers of investigators to launch their own enquiries could help overcome the problem of the significant numbers of cases that police fail to refer for investigation. The capacity of police to act as gatekeepers, preventing cases being scrutinised by external inspectors, is evident in research by the IPCC. A study of six PSDs found that approximately a fifth of cases that should have been mandatorily referred to the IPCC had not been, and that this included cases involving deaths and serious injuries, serious corruption and serious assaults (IPCC 2015). The same report found a lack of formal processes for determining which cases were referred to the IPCC and that staff with responsibility in this area lacked training and misunderstood the criteria for referring cases. In part this might reflect austerity cuts to police budgets, and the related political imperative to maintain 'frontline' services explains the lack of resources to 'backroom' PSDs. Research by Her Majesty's Inspector of Constabulary (HMIC 2014) found that 1 per cent of police staff in England and Wales in 2014 were employed in PSDs, a total of 2,043 staff, which meant an average service had around 47 staff engaged in complaints investigation (although the HMIC data included those involved in vetting and information security). In any event it is clear that the central role that police services themselves play in responding to complaints made against them continues to undermine full independent accountability. A study commissioned by the IPCC found a considerable lack of confidence in the impartiality of the investigation process and that this was a feature among police themselves, non-police stakeholders (community groups, for example) and even staff engaged in the accountability process (Populus 2016). Forty per cent of police surveyed were 'not very' or 'not at all' confident of the impartiality of the IPCC system, as were 30 per cent of non-police respondents and 24 per cent of stakeholders in the accountability process. It seems likely that these concerns might reflect different perceptions in the sense that police might feel that a lack of impartiality disadvantages them, while non-police parties might regard the problem in the other direction as being to the disadvantage of complainants. The challenge of reconciling different parties within police complaints systems was cited by Prenzler and Porter (2016) as a factor underpinning the widespread dissatisfaction with arrangements found in many countries, especially since competing claims might be irreconcilable. A zero-sum game operates such that providing a satisfactory outcome to one party might inevitably leave the other dissatisfied. Similarly, Torrible (2016) argued it is impossible to establish whether mechanisms are effective since there is a lack of consensus as to the primary purpose of complaints systems – which are variously identified as means to check abuses of power, or as an organisational learning tool, or as necessary to promote public legitimacy.

Concerns about perceived impartiality are further demonstrated in relation to the second element of new powers afforded to the IOPC: that officers have a legal duty to cooperate with investigations. Formally, it might be a relatively straightforward regulation, but much of the research on police occupational culture highlights the continuing difficulty of the 'blue curtain', such that internal solidarity among officers is an obstacle to whistle blowing or reporting the problematic behaviour of colleagues. A recurring theme in much of the research on police occupational culture is the strong bond of affinity between colleagues, such that group loyalty is a very high priority. Studies based on observational accounts of police officers on routine duty noted that officers always backed each other up and were constantly on the alert for potential danger (Banton 1964; Skolnick 1966; Cain 1973). Skolnick, for example, found that 'mainstream police culture is characterised by isolation, solidarity, suspiciousness and conservatism, all constructing a picture of a "symbolic assailant", threatening order and the police themselves' (cited in Reiner 2015: 319). As a consequence, there may be an unwillingness to report colleagues who violate the rules: this is the 'blue code of silence' that shrouds officers in the face of investigation from internal or external scrutineers (Westmarland 2005; Westmarland and Rowe 2018). Skolnick (1991) provides evidence of public inquiries and investigations that have uncovered police corruption, including examples of telling lies and extreme brutality where officers had seemed confident that the code of silence would protect them. He cites police violence against Rodney King in Los Angeles in 1991, and that those officers inflicting violence seemed unworried by the presence of police observers. Skolnick (1991: 7) argued that 'those who participated must have believed they could count on their colleagues to lie in case of an investigation'. As is outlined further in Chapter 6, many efforts to promote integrity and an ethical culture within policing have sought to address the cultural imperative officers often face not to report misconduct by colleagues. A core critique of police complaint processes in many jurisdictions has been that auto-investigations are compromised by the cultural affinity between the investigator, the subject of the inquiry and police witnesses. The development of mechanisms to promote independent investigations – either directly through employing non-police investigators, or indirectly through mechanisms for independent oversight and management of investigations – can be understood as attempts to overcome such limitations. In practice, this would improve the quality and fairness of investigations and enhance public confidence in the trust and legitimacy of complaint investigations. Quite how the new IOPC legal requirement for 'full' cooperation from police staff will be operationalised is difficult to conceptualise, and the legal or administrative processes required might be in tension with another stated goal, which is that the IOPC resolves complaints more quickly. Changes introduced in 2015 by the Home Office further widened the scope of complaints systems by creating a new category of 'super-complainants' – charities and other organisations who are able to bring cases relating to wider matters of public interest. The package of reforms included that internal disciplinary hearings be held in public, under the auspices of an independent legally qualified chair.

A further dimension in the remit of the IOPC is to promote organisational learning from complaints. As noted above, it is often claimed that police approaches to complaint investigation has assumed a formal disciplinary character and that this could usefully be transformed such that police services seek instead to learn lessons from complaints and regard these as organisational developmental opportunities. To this end the IOPC provides to police services and the public bulletins organised around key policing themes – custody, dealing with vulnerable people, use of DNA evidence, and so on – that distil learning points that have arisen from individual complaints. The bulletins also provide guidance on conducting investigations themselves, reflecting the role of the Office in promoting good practice across the sector. These can be considered 'soft power' instruments of police accountability and sit alongside myriad guidelines and directives emanating from other governance agencies discussed throughout this book. The status that they have in terms of informing police practice remains largely unknown; while police services are legally bound to report back to the IOPC to outline specific changes made following a particular complaints investigation, responding to the more generic 'learning the lessons' bulletins is at the discretion of police services.

Civil claims against police

In contrast to the formal complaints mechanisms outlined in the previous section, there is a lack of data relating to the extent of civil claims made against police in Britain, and so little reliable information about trends, patterns, outcomes and associated costs. The lack of research into this route to addressing alleged misconduct has been a noted cause for concern for some time. In 2011 Greater Manchester Police Authority (GMPA) (2011) revealed that the service had received 772 'letters of claim' for public liability cases (which 'predominantly relate to allegations of wrongful arrest/false imprisonment') for the period 2006/07 to 2010/11. Over the same period, the service had paid £1,186,500 in damages for such claims. In 2017 the Metropolitan Police Service (2017) reported that it had received 2,366 claims for 'malfeasance' over the period 2012/13 to 2016/17, and during the same period had settled 963 such claims and paid £15,589,025 in settlements. In neither police service did the data indicate that the number of cases or the value of settlements were increasing, but since not all services routinely provide information in a standard format it is not possible to assess any wider trends. A similar lack of data was noted in a review of civil litigation against police in Australia (McCulloch and Palmer 2007). The relative lack of attention paid to civil claims reflects and reinforces the impression that this form of accountability is an adjunct to the formal complaints system.

Data obtained via a freedom of information request submitted to all police services in England and Wales revealed a declining trend in the number of civil claims made between 2012 and 2017 (see Figure 4.1). Twenty-five police services responded to the request, reporting that they received a total of 3,043 claims in 2012, a figure that reduced to 2,447 by 2017, which might reflect changes in Legal Aid availability, as is outlined further below. Of those claims, 1,212 (40 per cent of

Figure 4.1: Civil claims against police, number of claims and number of substantiated claims, 2012–17

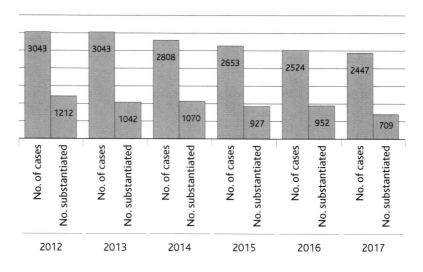

the total) were substantiated in 2012, a proportion that fell to 29 per cent for 2017.

Financial settlements for the 25 police services are shown in Table 4.1, which indicates payment of nearly £24 million over the six-year period.

Also uncertain is the capacity of civil claims to provide effective accountability of police. In terms of the various advantages that might derive from effective police complaints processes (to provide learning opportunities for the organisation, to redress public grievances and to deter abuse of power) it seems that civil action might have limited potential. Notably, police service responses to individual cases brought against them often state that 'lessons have been learnt' to improve future cases. One of the complaints noted in the GMPA (2011) report cited above was brought after a protestor had a mask forcibly removed during a political demonstration, which the court found to be illegal on the basis that protestor had not been wearing the mask to conceal her identity. GMPA reported that their public order training subsequently had been amended to reflect this ruling. While individual instances such as this might be significant, the lack of any oversight body in civil cases limits the wider capacity for police services more widely to be exposed to such teachable moments.

Research with legal representatives engaged in civil action against police has found that they tend to regard this form of address as a valuable means of accountability (Smith 2003; McCulloch and Palmer 2007). Although the effect in terms of deterring officer misconduct might be minimal (not least because in many jurisdictions officers are not personally liable), there have been numerous occasions on which civil action has led to public exoneration of those at the wrong end of police malpractice and that have led to significant changes to operational policing. As McCulloch and Palmer (2007: 85) noted: 'There is no doubt that at times civil litigation and particularly civil trials can provide an outlet for aggrieved citizens and for community scrutiny and judicial review of police behaviour and practices that would otherwise be hidden from public view.'

Nonetheless, while satisfaction might be achieved for the individual complainant, civil claims are less likely than judicial review to bring about change since they are primarily focused on officer wrongdoing

Table 4.1: Civil claims against the police, financial settlements, 2012–17

2012	2013	2014	2015	2016	2017
3,719,558.75	4,783,633.17	4,512,365.55	4,317,038.13	3,584,837.46	2,9743,22.65

rather than policy and process. A prime example of powerful judicial review recently in England and Wales relates to the action successfully brought against the Metropolitan Police by two victims of the serial rapist John Worboys. The court ruled in their favour on the basis that the failure of the police to effectively investigate the crimes against them amounted to a breach of their Article 3 human rights to protection against torture, inhuman or degrading treatment. The ruling[1] by the Supreme Court was significant because it reversed previous judgments that tended not to regard police as liable, especially when failed investigations were matters of operational mistakes by officers rather than systemic problems. The 2018 ruling established that the police have a duty to ensure that serious harms amounting to breaches of human rights are rigorously investigated and that operational failures amount to a breach of that duty. Clearly this is a prime example of means by which civil action against police can effect significant changes, and act as a powerful form of governance. Conaghan (2017: 76) argued that the case was part of an emerging trend whereby political campaigning and legal action could combine to provide effective mechanisms to shape police practice (issues returned to in Chapter 7): 'The case powerfully illustrates the potential of law as a site of contestation in which the political stakes extend well beyond the interests of the immediate parties. Litigation provides a crucial space for public discourse with the power to shape and inform public attitudes and beliefs.'

Conaghan's analysis demonstrates that civil action against police can provide accountability that impacts on the wider public interests as well as providing restitution for individual claimants. Nonetheless, she also indicates that social and political campaigning are also significant in determining the outcome of civil actions (they may, for example, facilitate fundraising to resource claims), which means that securing governance and accountability through such means is somewhat determined by the extent to which an individual complaint can secure wider public support. For these reasons, access to justice may be denied to those without the economic, political and social capital to bring claims.

This reflects a more general limitation of civil actions against police, particularly in the light of recent restrictions on Legal Aid and Jackson's (2009) official review of civil litigation costs, which led to reduced capacity for obtaining insurance in 'no win; no fee' cases and so increased risks for litigants. Smith's (2003) interviews with defence solicitors identified that access to public funding was a crucial factor in shaping their advice to clients considering civil action against the police. While in principle such funding continues to be available for action against police, it is means tested, and solicitors reported that they would not advise clients to pursue civil action if they had to rely on their own resources since they would become liable for the costs of both parties should they lose their case. In those circumstances the formal public complaints process outlined above was the recommended route. The financial risks involved in bringing civil action against police highlight wider concern that access to justice is effectively denied to those who lack the resources to fund action. This problem has been exacerbated by the Legal Aid, Sentencing and Punishment of Offenders Act 2012, which further restricted the provision of support for legal action and effectively lowered the financial threshold at which it is provided (Law Society 2017). As a mechanism to hold police to account, civil action is clearly limited if those without financial capacity are effectively precluded from bringing cases; a justice gap made worse since many of those, especially young people, most negatively affected by over-policing are precisely those less likely to be able to pursue this route.

The advice that those without access to Legal Aid to fund cases ought to revert to the police complaints system is problematic since Smith's (2003) study also found that an important factor motivating those seeking civil redress was a lack of confidence in that very system. He found that this particularly was related to perceptions that complaints were not subject to rigorous independent investigation. Other motivations to pursue civil action included the desire for public vindication following police wrongdoing. Smith (2003) found higher levels of satisfaction among those bringing civil claims against police compared to those entering grievances via the complaints system. In part, he found, this was attributable to their perception that they had greater control over the process as it unfolded, in relation to viewing evidence, managing timelines, and so forth. In terms of outcomes, successful complainants were most satisfied in terms of personal vindication, in the sense that they could demonstrate that they had not committed the criminal activity originally alleged. There was less confidence, however, that the resolution of their case led police to take action against officers involved or to learn lessons to inform future conduct. Although it is unclear from Smith's (2003) study on what basis the claimants might know of the consequences for officers or staff involved in their case, this perception suggests that the outcomes of civil litigation might be limited in terms of the broader capacity of complaints to provide learning opportunities for police services. Nonetheless, the Police Action Lawyers Group (PALG, a professional association of lawyers bringing civil actions against police) noted similarly that their clients tend to have priorities beyond financial compensation (PALG 2016: 3):

> Clients seek non-financial remedies such as a declaration of a violation of their rights, an apology or a change in policy. Their cases have wider significance to the public and serve to improve standards and practices within police forces and other public authorities. Without these cases many improper, discriminatory and unlawful practices would never be brought to light, culpable conduct would not be exposed and lessons would not be learned for the future.

Redressing complaints in the wider policing environment

While there are weaknesses in relation to investigating complaints against the police service, there are at least formal mechanisms, beyond the general remit of the law, in place to respond to citizen grievances. No parallel provisions exist in the UK in relation to the private security industry, or to the more complex networks through which policing activities are delivered. In terms of the private security industry in its broad range of activities, many of which involve direct interaction with the public as well as work with other companies and agencies, avenues to pursue complaints are very limited. Until relatively recently, private security in Britain was only loosely regulated. Prior to the Private Security Industry Act 2001, regulation was left to the market mechanism and the requirements imposed by voluntary membership of bodies such as the British Security Industry Authority (BSIA) and the International Private Security Association (IPSA). The BSIA and IPSA require that member companies comply with British Standards codes of practice relating to guarding and the installation of equipment. Other sectors, such as private investigators, remained largely unregulated. The apparent expansion of private security companies patrolling residential neighbourhoods, funded by local householders and businesses, means that encounters between public and policing agencies are subject to a formal complaints system in some circumstances, where the policing agency is the police, but not others, where the policing agency is a private security company. Private security companies might not embody state sovereignty and be bound up with legitimacy and authority in the same way as police, but in terms of their capacity to deliver symbolic or actual violence against members of the public they mirror the status of police. Formal arrangements in terms of private security personnel in Britain are primarily focused on the initial vetting of applicants and licensing those engaged in activities such as guarding property, protecting cash-in-transit and door supervision at licensed premises. Licences can be revoked, or not renewed, if the operative is subject to a criminal sanction for certain offences or if they are judged by the BSIA not to be a 'fit and proper' person. While the BSIA encourages reports of criminal behaviour that might affect the integrity of a licence holder, complaints of a non-criminal nature are the responsibility of the individual companies that employ them. The diversity of companies operating in private security is likely to mean that the internal mechanisms to respond to complaints made about staff will vary considerably, and in some cases it is likely that large-scale multinational corporations are likely to have relatively robust policies and processes capable of delivering procedurally just outcomes. Nonetheless, as was noted earlier in the chapter, there are a range of stakeholders to complaints systems and while the complainant and the subject of complaint might receive appropriate results, the private justice practised in this respect means that there is no scope for legitimacy to be enhanced by public transparency, and reduced scope for sector-wide organisational learning through this route.

White's (2016) contribution to the literature on accountability of private security draws attention to the wider spectrum, beyond the legal-formal arrangements outlined in this chapter, of mechanisms that can hold this sector to account, and some of the political processes he charts are discussed in later chapters of this book. Much of the argument developed later focuses on the multi-layered and variable forms of accountability that exist as forms of 'soft power' regulating officer behaviour from within and outside of the police organisation. As will be examined in Chapter 6, White (2016) uses the example of the 2012 London Olympics to illustrate how such pressures can impact on private security providers, regardless of formal or contractual arrangements. Important though it is to recognise other dimensions of accountability, it remains an obstacle to the legitimacy and authority of private security that there are not sector-wide arrangements to address public complaints about misconduct.

In the absence of such arrangements, complaints about private security personnel can only be addressed, as has been noted, directly through the companies that employ them or by reporting potential misconduct to the police. Recent news media stories have highlighted cases where private security companies have been offering street patrols in communities said to be left vulnerable in the face of a declining police presence. Often, in such reports, those offering such services emphasise that they are providing reassurance to anxious publics and their patrols are an effective deterrent. Over an extended period researchers have focused on the relation of private security to public police (Shearing and Stenning 1981; Johnston 1992; Crawford 2003) and in these representations private companies tend to present themselves as auxiliary services, subservient to the police service. In terms of accountability, the dominant position of public police is apparent, since they continue to investigate complaints from the public about private security staff. In Loader and Walker's (2007) terms, the police are the 'anchor' organisation providing oversight of private security companies, a role in tension with the 'partnership of equals'/ co-delivery model of police and private security cooperation that characterises contemporary networked policing. If public concerns about the actions of private security personnel mirror those about police then a considerable proportion will relate to behaviours that are not criminal in nature, but nonetheless are significant. Dominant narratives about antisocial behaviour, gangs, drug crime, street robbery and so forth are likely to inform the practices of security personnel, especially if they are seeking to address apparent public anxieties. In the context of shopping malls, Wakefield (2003) found private security staff made operational surveillance decisions that reflected established stereotypes that labelled some as potential 'problems' to be monitored. Although this might not lead to identifiably criminal misconduct – reportable to police – it is likely nonetheless to entail discrimination, marginalisation and the over-policing of those at the hard end of dominant modes of social sorting. Unsatisfactory though it is that complaints about such behaviour that arise in relation to police officers are not subject to more robust investigation, there is at least an opportunity for such concerns to be lodged. The lack of a parallel mechanism for private security staff not only denies restitution to individuals, it also means that there is a lack of robust data about trends and patterns in an increasingly important sector of policing. In the context of complaints against police, Prenzler and Porter (2016) argued that the competing interests of the various parties are not always reconcilable, and as such there can be an inherent dissatisfaction with outcomes. The lack of public stake in the investigation of complaints against private security companies removes the possibility of securing trust and legitimacy through this form of accountability. On this basis, the private security industry has no parallel with the role that the IPCC played in terms of improving public confidence in policing through promoting the transparency and independence of the complaints system.

Accountability for policing delivered by private security companies becomes more complex still in terms of work undertaken through contracts with the public police. In contrast with private security roles outlined earlier is the wide range of activities subcontracted by the police (and other public bodies with law enforcement functions, such as the Border Agency) to private companies. Early analysis of the role of private companies in the provision of police services often focused on the 'backroom' and support functions that were contracted out: maintenance and supply, training and personnel functions, for example (Jones and Newburn 1998). These might have been areas unlikely to occasion complaints from the public and so matters of relatively minor significance in terms of wider debates about accountability. As relations between private, third-sector and public police have developed, however, plural agencies are now routinely engaged in frontline policing activities that make the lack of accountability more problematic. The formal police complaints mechanisms outlined earlier in this chapter have incrementally extended to include new members of the 'extended police family' such as police community support officers and civilian staff. Similarly, new agencies beyond police constabularies, such as the NCA, the Gangmasters and Labour Abuse Authority and PCCs, have been incorporated into the accountability provided by the IOPC. Given this, it is anomalous that private security operating, for example, in custody suites or in immigration detention and removal raids are not subject to the same scrutiny. This accountability gap was highlighted in a Home Affairs Committee (2013b: 33) report that noted:

> The landscape of policing is changing and the IPCC must change with it. Increasingly, companies like G4S, Capita, Mitie and Serco are involved in delivering services that would once have fallen solely to the police ... yet the public cannot call on the IPCC to investigate their delivery of those services ... The Commission's jurisdiction should be extended to cover private sector contractors in their delivery of policing services and appropriate funding should be available for it to undertake all the functions which we consider it should have responsibility for.

This recommendation was endorsed by the IPCC itself (Home Affairs Committee 2013c: 21), although later legislation creating the IOPC did not incorporate this approach. One of the companies cited by the Committee, G4S, argued that since police legitimacy is enhanced by a robust independent mechanism for investigating complaints, the private security industry would similarly benefit (Home Affairs Committee 2013d: 4). The company also indicated that it had '… contractually included IPCC co-operation and compliance into our strategic partnership contract with Lincolnshire Police'. While this provides greater equity in governance arrangements, it relies on a bi-party local agreement and there remains no statutory requirement that this should extend more widely.

Conclusion

It has been argued that the nature of police work and the organisational culture of policing present significant challenges to effective complaints investigation and that this jeopardises the capacity of this form of accountability. Moreover, different parties to complaints investigation – police, complainant and wider public – might have irreconcilable interests that cannot all be satisfied by the outcome of the case. Combined with the range of types of complaint and the breadth of policing activities that might conceivably be addressed, these factors explain the widespread dissatisfaction surrounding police complaints investigations in many countries across considerable time periods (Prenzler and Porter 2016). To some extent, the research evidence reviewed above suggests that this dissatisfaction underpins complainants' decisions to pursue civil action against police. While there is a lack of reliable evidence on the nature and impact of such actions, it has been shown that there seems to have been a decrease in such claims over recent years, and a reduction in the value of settlements. While Smith (2003) suggested that solicitors bringing civil action felt that this was an effective mechanism that could bring change to operational police practice, as is illustrated in relation to the judgment in the case brought by victims of John Worboys, it is difficult to identify this since there is a lack of robust evidence. Establishing the public interest benefit of civil claims is difficult given this gap.

Similarly, private security companies are only minimally held to account for the conduct of their personnel. While the BSIA has a role in terms of the initial licensing and subsequent renewal of operators working in some security roles, this does not extend to significant areas such as patrol work, and is only focused on criminal behaviour – other unacceptable activities are not covered. These gaps are only loosely filled by arrangements for in-house investigations by companies themselves. Although this might be robust is some cases, there is little external oversight and the industry loses an opportunity to gain public legitimacy associated with a more independent and transparent model. It is anomalous that private security staff are not subject to the same oversight measures as their public police counterparts, even in circumstances where they are performing the same roles and engaging in the same way with the public.

In relation to formal complaints, civil claims and cases applying to the private sector, weaknesses and loopholes have been identified. Additional to these is the inherent limitation of accountability measures that are focused on the alleged misconduct of individual staff acting beyond legal or normative standards of behaviour. Considering public grievances against police in terms of the conduct of individual officers provides no safeguard or restitution in respect of policing operations or tactics that are formally compliant with legal and organisational codes but are nonetheless controversial and resented by significant sections of the population. Smith (2006) argued that the roots of contemporary arrangements to respond to complaints about police developed from police resistance to accountability in England and Wales in the 1970s, which was couched in terms of the need to protect 'operational independence'. This meant, he argued, that concessions in the light of public concern about police activity (relating to racism or public disorder, see IRR 1979; Scarman 1981) were always in the domain of enhancing the complaints system rather than other forms of governance. This reflects a 'bad apples' approach, such that police malpractice is attributed to the misconduct of recalcitrant individuals rather than any organisational or institutional problem. Other measures of accountability apply in relation to practices such as stop and search, the policing of football supporters or those 'kettled' while demonstrating, but these 'meso-level' matters of operational police practice are not formally addressed by the macro-level accountability measures described in Chapter 3 or by those outlined in this chapter. Some of these other arrangements, formal and informal, internal and external, are addressed in the chapters that follow.

Note

1   *Commissioner of Police of the Metropolis v DSD* UKSC 2015/0166.

Further reading

Smith, G. (2006) 'A Most Enduring Problem: Police Complaints Reform in England and Wales', *Journal of Social Policy*, 35(1): 121–41.

Torrible, C. (2016) 'Reconceptualising the Police Complaints Process as a Site of Contested Legitimacy Claims', *Policing and Society: An International Journal of Research and Policy*, DOI: 10.1080/10439463.2016.1191486.

Wakefield, A. (2003) *Selling Security*, Cullompton: Willan.

5

Science, evidence and police accountability in the age of big data

This chapter explores the impact that the increasing use of data and science have on policing in terms of the organisation and delivery of police responses to crime and crime prevention. The use of scientific evidence to develop improved policing services offers many advantages, especially in a period where demands on the public police are transformed by technological change, and resources available to meet new challenges have reduced in absolute terms. The use of science to promote EBP and the related but distinct development of 'big data policing' generally have not been thought of as means to control police discretion. Nonetheless, it is argued here that both provide powerful opportunities to reorient behaviour and practice, and their growing significance in contemporary policing means that is of vital importance to consider the implications that they have in terms of democratic accountability and public oversight. Both EBP and big data policing represent futures of policing that are difficult, although not necessarily impossible, to reconcile with established systems of 'hard' accountability outlined in the previous chapters of this book.

Evidence-based policing, professionalisation and police accountability

Unlike other recent shifts in police styles and practices – such as 'hot spots', 'intelligence-led' or 'problem-oriented' policing – EBP is best understood not as a model of delivery but as a strategy for improving effectiveness and efficiency. Drawing on the wider approaches to evidence-based policy within public administration, EBP offers the potential to transform established tradition, custom and practice in police work through the application of scientific research and evaluation. As is widely noted, police work has tended to be responsive in the sense that it is reactive to incidents once they have occurred, and organised around traditional models of patrol that are, to some extent, predicated on public demand for visible policing. It was noted in Chapter 1 that it is in this environment that police officers exercise their individual discretion as they discharge their complex and wide-ranging duties. Concerns about holding officers to account in this environment have broadly been reactive too, seeking to redress problems and complaints once they are raised. Higher-level governance, provided by networks of central and local agencies, is predicated on the general democratic principle that the public, being subject to laws, ought to be their author, as Rousseau (1762/1968) argued. Both EBP and big data policing are strategies that raise significant challenges in terms of democratic accountability since their credibility is derived from techno-scientific processes that might be in tension with public demand and are difficult to hold to account in technical terms.

Evidence-based policing has developed in many jurisdictions (including the UK, US, New Zealand and Singapore) as part of a broader process of professionalisation. Sherman (2013) characterises EBP as the replacement of the traditional '3 Rs model' of policing (delivered on the basis of random patrol, rapid response and reactive investigations) with a 'triple-T' using scientific approaches to target police activity, test the impact and track the long-term effect of particular types of intervention. Within the UK, research organisations incorporating police and academic researchers have been established, including the Scottish Institute for Policing Research, the N8 Policing Research Partnership of northern universities and police services, the Universities' Police Science Institute based at Cardiff University and the East Midlands Policing Academic Collaboration (Goode and Lumsden 2018). The Society of Evidence-Based Policing operates in the UK with the 'aim to make evidence based methodology part of every-day policing' and has partner organisations in Canada, the US and Australia. As the Society's website indicates, EBP aims to reorient police work through the application of scientific practice, innovation and evaluation to policing problems. Through the use of scientific analysis, innovation and experimentation, research and evaluation it is intended that policing is transformed from a craft practice to a profession, a key characteristic of which is the link to a corpus of evidence that informs practice. It was in these terms that Neyroud (2011) advocated that policing ought to be professionalised, a process that he also argued entailed developing a body to accredit officers and regulate professional practice. To a large extent this is the role that the College of Policing has come to adopt in England and Wales, through, for example, the development of Authorised Professional Practice (APP). APPs establish standards for police practice that are developed by a Guidance Committee on the basis of scientific evidence gleaned by systematic reviews with advice from subject matter experts, academics and specialist practitioners.

Closely aligned with the development of EBP is a renewed emphasis on police undertaking higher education. The relation to EBP is, in part, a response to concerns that police staff who might be engaged in innovation, evaluation and EBP often do not have the capacity to reflect properly on the challenges of operational implementation; and that officers involved in operational implementation will often not grasp the value, significance or, indeed, the potential limitations of scientific research in policing (Crawford 2017). Improving police professionalism through higher education has been a recurring project since Augustus Vollmer, chief of Los Angeles police a century ago and known as the 'father of professional policing', advocated that all officers be required to complete three years of university-level study (Polk and Armstrong 2001). Holdaway (2017) has argued that the 're-professionalisation' of policing, a term he prefers on the basis that current developments restate earlier claims to professional status through the creation of the College and the nurturing of a canon of scientific evidence to inform practice, represents a new regulatory framework. In this new model, he argued, governance is at a distance from ministers as it is practised relatively independently by the police service itself. As Holdaway (2017) noted, the role of the College in developing and promoting an evidential base of 'what works' in policing might be in tension with other actors in the diverse framework of accountability. PCCs, in particular, are distinguished in this environment by their democratic mandate, even if this might be a problematic and challenged source of authority, such that they can insist that policing is delivered according to public demand, regardless of any basis in evidence. Professional practice, promulgated by the College and rooted in scientific analysis, might be in tension with public demand, as in respect of the provision of visible foot patrols, for example. Sherman (2013: 382) argued that the College and police researchers would provide grounds to arbitrate between competing democratic demands through 'setting independent, evidence-based standards of police practice'. Moreover, Sherman (2009) has argued that experimental criminology is important in the promotion of the liberty of the citizen and has strong democratic credentials. Improving the evidential basis for criminal justice and social policy will, he argued, strengthen the liberty of the citizen by reducing the likelihood that individual freedom will be breached by criminal activity. The outcomes of policing experiments advocated by Sherman (2013) seem likely to be problematic, however, since they are conducted in a social context in which crime and disorder are not randomly distributed. Hope (2009: 130–1, and further to Rosenbaum 2007) reminds that 'if technology is the driving force that dictates policing strategies and tactics, then intelligence-led policing directed at crime hotspots will more or less certainly (especially in the US context) direct police to the street-corners of the ghetto'. The social, political and economic impacts of technically neutral policing are reconsidered later in relation to big data policing. As Sherman (2013) has acknowledged elsewhere, it is simplistic to assume that 'evidence' will be applied to policing in ways that are value free or without political or ideological interference. Even in circumstances where operational practice is delivered fully on the basis of scientific evidence, the identification of policing priorities will continue to be informed by a dominant understanding of the aetiology of crime and political and economic structures that contribute to criminalisation of marginalised communities and behaviour.

It is not only for overtly political or methodological reasons that the capacity of EBP to deliver enhanced professional practice is limited. The relation between EBP and democratic accountability is paradoxical for a number of reasons. In many respects, tension between professionalism (which relies on the use of scientific practice) and democratic authority are the central ambiguity that Sklansky (2008) identifies at the heart of police professionalism. He noted that demands for professional policing are often positively couched in terms of improved effectiveness, reduced violence and greater ethics, but that they have often been seen as inimical to democratic policing that meets community expectations. He noted a more negative history, associated in the US in particular with police being remote from the public. Similarly, in England and Wales in the 1960s the development of unit beat policing and motorised patrol were underpinned by the need for professional efficiency (Rawlings 2005: 200) but were subsequently linked to declining public engagement that necessitated a 'return' to community policing. Waddington (1999: 207) argued that advocacy of community policing in England and Wales in the 1970s can only be properly understood as rejection of the technocratic professionalism of policing that had occurred in England and Wales during the late 1960s. Similarly, Sklansky (2008) illustrated how in New York in the 1980s police professional analysis of the illegal drug trade de-prioritised conducting raids at apartment blocks, but that this caused tension with residents who demanded such responses. More recently, Leicestershire Police conducted an experiment whereby SOCOs were only sent to selected victims of domestic burglary in order to establish whether there was any effect in terms of solving cases and bringing offenders to court (BBC 2015). While the results suggested little evidential value arose from dispatching SOCOs, practices were not changed due to public concerns (expressed in the media, by the PCC and a local MP) that victims were not getting sufficient levels of service. In an era where realist ontology and claims of scientific certainty are challenged through alt-right denigration of 'experts' and the cry of 'fake news' makes 'truth' and 'evidence' inherently suspect concepts, it might be difficult to reconcile EBP with populist demands in terms of police priorities and styles. As is developed further in Chapter 8, a lack of public trust in government – noted as problematic in the development of community policing in post-conflict societies (Goldsmith 2005) – might become an increasing challenge for EBP in a 'post-truth' world.

In other respects, the paradoxical relation between EBP and democratic accountability is such that political pressures exerted by national and local agencies can curtail the capacity of police and researchers to develop a scientific basis for police action. Goode and Lumsden (2018) record views of police staff engaged in research who note that pressures of austerity have reduced capacity to develop scientific data and restricted, in cultural terms, the appetite for senior managers to undertake experimental work that may 'fail'. Sherman (2015: 20) argued that accepting that less than optimal outcomes might be achieved is central to the promotion of EBP since it is inherent to the scientific process:

> Nothing could be more important than for the police culture to learn this lesson: in science, we must let chips fall where they may. The crucible for this value is reacting to research findings that contradict national policy or even law. Even if evidence is not altered or suppressed, the smothering paradigm of 'national policy' may cause the evidence to be ignored. The best vaccine for this problem is to educate the culture of a police agency to understand and appreciate science.

In a period of austerity or, as in earlier periods in policing in UK, under the terms of New Public Management demands for efficiency and effectiveness, it seems likely that scientific principles will be difficult to embed into conservative and risk-averse police environments. It is noted later that organisational arrangements and a lack of technological capacity have meant that the potential of big data policing has not been realised in the UK (Babuta 2017), and these are bound up with resources and governance pressures. Furthermore, the pressure to conform to political priorities – which might be entirely legitimate in the exercise of police governance – impose internal policing priorities that are potentially at odds with the evidence base. Coupled with organisational constraints is the cultural propensity for police officers to apply EBP in short-term and shallow ways that demonstrate successful outcomes that are useful for career progression. That experiments and innovative practice are 'doomed to succeed' in the sense that positive outcomes will inevitably be identified in the context of sponsoring officers with career ambitions was noted as a barrier to EBP in Fleming and Wingrove's (2017) study, alongside organisational and resource limitations. Among these latter factors is the hierarchical nature of police leadership, such that officers are inhibited in the development of innovative practice and evaluation, some of which are rooted in a tradition of 'disciplinary' codes intended to ensure effective governance and oversight. In this context, there are tensions and contradictions between formal accountability to organisational rules and structures and accountability to scientific evidence that informs effective police practice. Goode and Lumsden (2018: 81) identified an 'organisational culture characterised by calls for accountability, the pervasiveness of performance management and measurement, and a proliferation of bureaucratic systems as a form of micromanagement'. Such features are intended to promote compliance with established political frameworks but inhibit the expert practice of policing and the development of scientific evidence core to professionalism.

To some extent, the tension between policing that is accountable to democratic oversight and policing that is accountable to scientific evidence can be reconciled. Since scientific research will often not produce an unambiguous template for police action there remains a need to determine police priorities and strategies in relation to broader democratic norms determined through the networks of police accountability outlined in Chapter 3. Furthermore, those agencies and stakeholders in accountability networks can commission scientific research to further the priorities that they seek to address on the basis of their democratic mandate. In the case of the College of Policing, for example, the creation of an evidence base for policing is overseen by independent experts and stakeholders from the broader 'family' of police governance actors. In this way there is scope to develop EBP that reflects Argyrous's (2012) model for improving evidence and policy making through ensuring that the process by which it is generated is open and transparent. Among the criteria for achieving this, he argued, are the need to ensure that methodological and theoretical assumptions underpinning research are explicitly stated, and that there is open access to raw data gathered in the experimental process. Even though the development of scientific evidence can itself be subject to democratic accountability, there remains the inherent conundrum that applies to all evidence-based policy making. Fundamentally, the tension surrounding EBP and police professionalism is that between the principle that the police officer is a citizen in uniform, responding to public demands expressed through legal and political mechanisms, and a model of the professional technocratic cop acting dispassionately on the basis of scientific knowledge that remains opaque to the public at large. Put simply the question becomes: should police be accountable to the public via political authorities or accountable to science and evidence? A further significant challenge to the EBP project is the inherent political, cultural, social and normative subjectivity in which much policing is bound up. While science can inform the development of more effective responses to particular problems such as domestic burglary, it does not provide inevitably unambiguous solutions to contentious policing challenges. The mandate of policing is such that some outcomes will be experienced as negative by some in society, and some aspects of policing – the policing of political demonstrations for example – even if conducted on the basis of best evidence, inevitably raise questions about civil liberties, free expression and public safety – which are not wholly amenable to scientific analysis. Fundamentally, if the role of police is to promote the 'public good' then inevitably this leads to discussion of normative or ethical standards against which policing outcomes are held to account, and these are not overridden by a technical judgement about 'what works' in policing (Morrell and Rowe 2019).

Algorithms, big data and 'machine policing'

The impact of big data extends increasingly across political, social and economic life and raises significant concerns about democracy, privacy, civil liberties and accountability. The term 'big data' is not clearly defined but tends to be used to connote not only the vast quantities of digital information, but also the technological ability to process information in real time. As in other fields, big data transforms the traditional gathering and processing of information or 'intelligence' (referred to by James 2016 as 'little data') that has always been central to policing and criminal justice. Kitchin (2014: 68–9) suggested that the world has entered an era of the 'zettabyte' (2^{70} bytes), since one calculation suggests that the world has generated 1.2 zettabytes of data.

Another illustration of the rise of big data is provided by the claim from the chairman of Google that the world generates as much data every two days as was created from the beginning of recorded human history until 2003 (Joh 2014). It is not just the sheer extent of digital information that characterises big data, however, and Kitchin (2014) identified key features as being:

- huge in volume;
- high in velocity (created in near real time);
- diverse in variety;
- exhaustive in scope (seeking information on the entire population);
- fine grained in resolution and indexical;
- relational with common fields enabling conjoining of different datasets;
- flexible (new fields can be added), and scalable (can expand in size).

In the context of police work, big data offers the potential to transform routine operational procedures, crime prevention and investigation. Crowd control, for example, can be informed by analysing real-time data generated from information gleaned from apps on smart phones that reveal the location and direction of individuals, as well as their social interactions and communications (see Chen et al 2016). Assemblages of similar data can reveal traffic flow, roadside parking and noise and air pollution, and can be used to sense the mood of gathered crowds (Zhu et al 2016). While social media was analysed as part of the police response to the London riots in 2011 (Procter et al 2013), in big data models policing is informed by the metadata gleaned from smart phone apps that reveal information not consciously shared by owners. Problematically, the reliability of such approaches has been questioned, such as when facial recognition software wrongly identified almost 2,300 people attending the EUFA Champions League final in Cardiff in 2017 as being wanted criminals – meaning that 92 per cent of 'matches' were wrong (BBC 2018). More positively, a review of the state of big data practice in UK policing identified four key ways in which potential could be better tapped (Babuta 2017: vii):

> First, predictive crime mapping could be used to identify areas where crime is most likely to occur …
>
> Second, predictive analytics could also be used to identify the risks associated with particular individuals …
>
> Third, advanced analytics could enable the police to harness the full potential of data collected through visual

surveillance, such as CCTV images and automatic number plate recognition (ANPR) data …

Fourth, big data technology could be applied to open-source data … which would ultimately inform the development of preventive policing strategies.

Each of these four applications raises concerns about police accountability and democracy, let alone for operational practice if the Champions League example indicates that the third element might be difficult to achieve. As is developed later, the nature of actuarial prediction and the construction and processing of data – especially open source data – using algorithms mean that current 'disproportionalities' in the delivery of policing are likely to be exacerbated. Young people and some minority groups who are already over-policed will become subject to ever further focus due to what Harcourt (2007) referred to as the 'ratchet' effect. Keats Citron and Pasquale (2014) considered the social, ethical and legal implications of a 'scored society' in which big data is used pervasively to rank and sort individuals for a broad range of purposes, including 'whether we are good credit risks, desirable employees, reliable tenants, valuable customers-or deadbeats, shirkers, menaces, and "wastes of time"' (2014: 1). They note that such technologies are often heralded as beneficial since they rely on apparently neutral and objective actuarial data but that in practice such sets are aggregated information that reflect the inaccuracies and biases of individual human beings. Ultimately, they argue, 'crucial opportunities are on the line, including the ability to obtain loans, work, housing, and insurance. Though automated scoring is pervasive and consequential, it is also opaque and lacking oversight' (Keats Citron and Pasquale 2014: 1). The basis of this opacity is threefold, Burrell (2016, cited in Lepri et al 2018: 619–20) suggested. Intellectual property rights holders intentionally obscure the details of valuable software and programming but this is combined with the illiterate opacity caused by a lack of public technical knowledge and the intrinsic opacity of 'deep learning' machine models.

It might be possible for democratic oversight mechanisms to develop to ensure that the tools and methods of big data policing are subject to public scrutiny, but – as was identified in Chapters 2 and 3 of this book – they would have to be significantly transformed since governance, ethics and accountability largely continue to be oriented to policing practices that developed in the 19th century. Any effort to instigate new approaches that control police algorithms and the mechanics of open source data would need to overcome the challenge of regulating multinational software corporations. Self-learning machines developing and adapting algorithms autonomously are inherently difficult to hold to account. In the military, Keats Citron and Pasquale (2014) note that the potential risks of deploying 'killer robots' capable of deploying lethal force against targets identified by an algorithm are mitigated by retaining a 'human-in-the-loop' able to exercise contextual judgement. Similar precautions need to be embedded as police deploy similar technologies. Akin to Argyrous's (2012) model for effective EBP, which combines multiple methods and perspectives and a transparent approach, Lepri et al (2018) argue that technology can provide solutions to the lack of transparency associated with the use of algorithms. They outlined a process of vetting such that 'algorithms should be verified by experts, policy makers, citizens to be as free as possible from biases and unintended side effects such as discrimination' (Lepri et al 2018: 623). Using such an approach in the face of the three strands of opacity that Burrell (2016) outlined remains challenging, as Lepri and colleagues acknowledged, and requires political, legal and industry commitment that is difficult to generate in a globally complex technocratic environment. These challenges are returned to later.

While the UK might be slow to adopt big data policing it is clear that policing practices have been significantly changed in the US and that important matters of democracy and accountability have emerged. Established policing practices such as crime mapping and profiling, practised since the 1990s using GIS software and the Compstat system associated with the 'blue revolution' and the 'crime drop' in New York city during that decade, are transformed through the use of big data. Predictive policing has been introduced in US cities using complex algorithms to mine police data and open source information to identify future places where crime will occur and those at risk of victimisation and of becoming offenders. A report in *Vice* magazine noted the potential for algorithms to analyse sonic data relating to urban shootings such that the correlation of certain sounds could enable the identification of precursor noises associated with gun fire, opening the possibility of police being deployed for preventive purposes (Vice 2014). Using AI and big data in that way might not yet be commonplace, but there are other examples of their routine use in contemporary operational practice. For example, Joh (2014) outlined how AI and risk terrain theory underpin predictive policing in New Jersey. Using crime data and information about local highways, the geographic concentration of young men and the location of hotels and apartment complexes, police have better targeted prevention and detection leading to significant reductions in violent and property crime. Another form of big data policing uses algorithms to profile social networks and identify central and peripheral actors involved in criminal gangs. Joh (2014: 47) outlined the transformative power this gives to police:

> While traditional police work might easily identify leaders within a criminal organization, social network analysis can identify those with influence or those who transmit information within the group quickly and yet whose roles are not otherwise apparent. The software can even reveal deliberately concealed affiliations. Even if an individual suspected of being part of a criminal organization does not admit his affiliation, social network software can calculate the probability of his membership.

As has been argued in relation to 'small data' traditional policing, however, identifying membership of criminal organisations is problematic in the context of dynamic loose connections of individuals, and stereotyping and labelling can lead to criminalisation. Although software might reveal otherwise concealed affiliations it seems probable that big data analysis is likely to be directed only at those pre-identified as gangs or organised crime groups of some kind, and that has tended to be understood in ways that reflect, among other things, the criminalisation and racialisation of minority ethnic groups. Cockbain's (2013) study of 'Asian sex gangs' engaged in the UK in the grooming of children found that understanding the problem of sexual offences against children in 'ethnic' terms reflects wider racist stereotypes and risks misdirecting investigations. Similarly, in a different context, Gunter (2016) argued that the street gang label is unfairly applied to black youth identified with street-based lifestyles and urban cultures, and that they and their friendship networks become subject to unfair police targeting. While it might be that big data analysis reveals hitherto unknown sets of relationships that disturb established preconceptions, it seems more likely (given that resource constraints will limit the application of the software technology) that big data will provide an apparently scientific authority to enhance established forms of targeting. Existing disproportionalities would become further entrenched.

Recent controversies about the impact of social media and 'fake news' in both the 2016 US presidential elections and the UK Brexit referendum were focused on the ways in which corporations, governments and political campaigners process data harvested from the personal information of millions of citizens. Clearly, such concerns extend to policing since many of the algorithms incorporate open source and social media data to detect and prevent offending. Technically, it might be that individual users of social media permit companies to process and sell their personal data but it is clear that many do not provide informed consent since the scope and extent of this reuse is not understood. Similarly, as Zhu et al (2016) demonstrated, users of smart phone apps tend inadvertently not to activate privacy controls and so allow access to unknown agencies, companies, criminal or terrorist networks. Such security vulnerabilities are yet to be fully understood in relation to the 'internet of things'. In the UK, police and intelligence services have legal power to access internet and social media data and records. While the content of individuals' online activity cannot be accessed, details of websites visited, social media and phone contacts can be accessed. Although the law provides this narrow safeguard of individual privacy, the capacity of big data algorithms to identify correlations in forms of behaviour and details of social networks on a vast scale means that profiles of particular people can still emerge. Similarly, in the US and the UK, legal guarantees of privacy mean that police are restricted (without a specific warrant) to collecting metadata relating to online and phone activity, rather than to monitoring the actual content of communications. However, personal relationships and behaviour might still become apparent. For example, the ability to geo-locate cell phones very precisely, to within a few feet, means that law enforcement agencies have been able to identify and find offenders even where there is no other evidence relating to their behaviour or association with others. Ferguson (2017) cites several examples where police have used software to identify phones found to be in close proximity to repeat crimes, leading to the apprehension of offenders. That civil liberty provisions to protect privacy are very weak in practice is also illustrated in his analysis, since secondary information gathered from online searches often allows the identification of an individual associated with a particular phone number. Moreover, metadata can reveal interesting patterns of behaviour that might arouse suspicion: for example, an individual calling hydrophonic stores, 'head shops', locksmiths and hardware stores might, Ferguson (2017: 112–13) argued, be preparing to grow marijuana.

Other concerns about the impact that big data might have on relations between police and citizens, and the accountability of police, relate to the central role that algorithms play in directing emerging strategy and tactics. Particularly when developed to be self-learning forms of AI, algorithms are controversial in the sense that they identify correlations between forms of behaviour that might prove invaluable in the prevention or detection of a particular crime but which might also, on occasion, be unhelpful, entirely spurious or even socially harmful. These limitations are particularly acute since proponents of big data policing (including the companies selling software and related technology) advocate that the model is more effective and efficient than human decision making and is an ethically and morally neutral exercise in statistical certainty. There are a number of reasons to doubt such claims. First, the research evidence is clear that the use of algorithms to detect offending behaviour (either past or future) is flawed in terms of the quality and veracity of the information contained in the databases. Quality and veracity are related but separate challenges. The quality of the data might be questionable in the sense that only partial or incomplete information might be provided and that this might mean that subsequent correlations identified by algorithms are 'false positives'. The location of complaints made about antisocial behaviour on a public transport network, for example, might show a spike in reports at a particular terminus and location details logged in the database. In practice, though, this would be a poor quality indicator if the greater number of incidents is explained by the nearby presence of a police station, meaning that the reports of experiences elsewhere on the network are made in that location and there is not actually greater prevalence there. Concerns about the veracity of data are subtly different in that they refer to false rather than incomplete information. If prejudiced commuters on the same public transport system are more likely to report concerns about particular groups that they wrongly associate with antisocial or criminal activity then false information is likely to enter the database and skew subsequent analysis.

The second related set of concerns refers to the lineage and provenance of data, and the lack of capacity for end users of AI- and algorithm-based policing to check how information has been transformed into intelligence and then into data, and by whom. While there are clear rules about continuity of evidence in other forms of criminal justice, there may be no parallel in respect of big data policing. This is particularly concerning since research evidence indicates that unintentional bias is a core feature of data coding, such that the lack of gender and ethnic representation among computer coders results in errors. This is problematic, for example, for facial recognition software, which, Garvie and Frankle (2016) noted, tends to mis-identify or not identify African Americans compared to other groups. This is a component of the wider problem identified by Harcourt (2007) in his argument against risk assessment and actuarial prediction. His analysis unravels the conceit that technical statistical analysis is inherently neutral and value free. Since police data reflects the bias inherent in operational practice, focused, as it is, disproportionately on certain crime types, particular locations and marginalised sections of the community, it is inevitable that the resulting information inputted into databases is skewed and partial. As noted earlier, Harcourt argued that a 'ratchet effect' occurred whereby the over-representation of some groups in police practice leads, through actuarial practice, to a spiral of increasing control and disproportionate police attention in ways that do not reflect crime patterns in society. He noted (2007: 190):

> The criminal law is by no means a neutral set of rules. It is a moral and political set of rules that codifies social norms, ethical values, political preferences, and class hierarchies. The use of actuarial methods serves only to accentuate the ideological dimensions of the criminal law. It hardens the purported race, class, and power relations between certain offences and certain groups.

While these are problems inherent in actuarialism they are exacerbated when self-learning algorithms conduct the analysis and identify correlations that reflect bias. If police disproportionally arrest black youths for marijuana use, for example, then the algorithm will identify correlation between ethnicity and offending even if marijuana use is as prevalent among ethnic groups not subject to over-policing (Ferguson 2017). While one response to this problem has been to remove ethnicity as a field in databases, as, for example, Durham Police have done in the UK, there remains the concern that 'proxy' indicators, such as postcode, will effectively continue to embed these disproportionalities into algorithmic policing. There are parallels here with police and media practices in earlier periods, before big data arrived, when place names ('Brixton', 'Toxteth' or 'Handsworth' in the UK) were used as synonyms for minority groups and so discussion of crime or social problems could continue to refer to race in coded terms (Keith 1993).

A further problem for big data policing is that it does not necessarily provide solutions to crime and disorder challenges, even when those are correctly identified. If problems of gun crime are identified through algorithmic analysis in particular districts of Chicago, as Crawford and Calo (2016) found, it does not follow that effective or acceptable solutions can be developed. In that case, greater police resources were deployed in the areas identified as hot spots but this led to no discernible reduction in gun crime and only increased tension with the local community. As with 'hot spots' policing, there are significant social, political and economic risks associated with the criminalisation of districts and populations that are already marginalised and disadvantaged and so the social and ethical ramifications of big data policing need to be addressed.

These problems highlight the wider challenge of developing big data policing in ways consistent with broader principles of democracy. The inherent biases associated with algorithms in policing are associated with disproportionality and the criminalisation of sections of the community. Democratically this is problematic, especially if police practice is contrary to civil rights, privacy and equality legislation. In such circumstances, policing becomes procedurally unjust, which will have a negative impact on public legitimacy. As the recent Black Lives Matter movement in the US has demonstrated, the police in such circumstances create and re-create boundaries of community and political inclusion that both reflect and sustain broader patterns of inequality in society.

For those reasons, holding big data policing to account is particularly important, but also especially challenging. First among the problems is that the software and technology that constitute algorithms tend to be created and owned by private IT companies which retain intellectual property rights and tend to be resistant – on commercial grounds – to external analysis of the coding. Kroll et al (2017) proposed a model whereby algorithms are regulated and required to meet certain industry standards, and this could provide safeguards against coding bias, and Crawford and Calo (2016) propose greater community transparency in shaping the scope of big data policing and the operational outcomes. Similar to proposals identified earlier that EBP can be made accountable if the methods and data applied are authored and monitored by external experts and stakeholders, there is potential to promote accountability through ensuring transparency and openness in the use of algorithms in policing. How this can be achieved, and by whom, is difficult to determine, however. Ferguson (2017) found that legislators are unable to penetrate the working of algorithms, and the fast-pace development of technology risks making legislation and post hoc legal challenges redundant. External scrutiny is even more problematic when algorithms are self-learning and relatively autonomous from governance and accountability, and when they draw on multiple streams of data, some of which is open source and some of which is of dubious provenance, the possibility of oversight becomes especially challenging.

Recognising the social and organisational context of EBP and big data policing

There are, however, a few caveats to this review of the negative features of big data policing and the difficulties of holding algorithms to account. First, there is no doubt that many benefits can be accrued from better understanding crime patterns, and clearly the application of such methods can help tackle crime. Predictive policing has the potential to reduce the social harm, human misery and economic costs associated with crime – costs that often weigh more heavily on those already experiencing marginalisation and relative deprivation. Used well, such approaches might enable the better identification of those at risk of crimes that might otherwise tend to be under-recognised or to help identify patterns and trends that can inform innovative and more effective responses. Recognising patterns in domestic abuse, for example, might allow for better risk profiling and the development of early interventions that prevent recurrence and the escalation of the gravity of the harm done to the victim.

A second caveat is the need to avoid technological determinism. It might not be – for political and economic reasons, for example – that the scope of big data in policing will be realised to the full extent of the technological potential. Policing in England and Wales remains fragmented, and national standard setting by the College of Policing and HMICFRS, for example, is mediated by local priorities. Chapters 2 and 3 showed that principles and practices of police governance are networked and there is no clear 'guiding hand' that might push big data to a pre-eminent role. Paradoxically, while EBP and big data strategies are often promoted as resource-efficient routes to achieving 'more with less', considerable investment in hardware, software, and expert IT professionals to engineer new systems and platforms, and continuing austerity measures, might render such investments unacceptable, especially given the political priority to protect frontline services. Even if EBP and big data policing develops incrementally at different paces in different places it need not be the case that it assumes a master role that determines all operational practice. Instead, algorithms and data analysis seem likely to be *an* influence rather than the *controlling* influence on policing. While this does not erase concerns about governance, ethics and accountability, it serves as a reminder that policing innovations are introduced into existing contexts, and that there are many examples of sharp new models being blunted by organisational structures, political inertia and occupational cultural resistance.

More widely, beyond policing, the need to avoid technological determinism is highlighted by Zietwitz's (2016) critical overview and partial check on debates that algorithms are 'taking over'. He reminds that algorithms should not be 'fetishized' as agential governing entities. For all the debate about the power and dominance of algorithms in diverse areas of contemporary life, there remains a stark lack of an agreed definition. On that basis, Zietwitz (2016: 4) cautions:

> Against this backdrop, claims about governing algorithms deserve some scrutiny and skepticism: how to account for the recent rise of algorithms as both a topic and a resource for understanding a wide range of activities? What challenges do algorithms pose for scholars in science and technology studies … and in the sociology, history, and anthropology of science and technology? And, yes, what actually is an algorithm?

A final caveat is that for all the limitations and caution about the application of EBP and big data to law enforcement and crime investigation, any potential that such approaches might bring in predictive terms could also be applied in ways that further accountability. As is discussed further in Chapter 6, internal management and people development techniques are focused, in part, on early identification of officers who might pose a risk in terms of using excessive force, generating citizen complaints, behaving corruptly and so forth. Through identifying patterns of associated behaviour that have been found to correlate with problematic actions, big data might help guide interventions that avert problems. In keeping with other models of predictive policing based on analysis of data sets, such potential might be partial and should be treated cautiously; nonetheless, algorithms should not be treated solely as a challenge in terms of accountability and governance.

Conclusion

Both evidence-based and big data policing strategies offer the prospect of delivering police work based on rigorous scientific research, producing outcomes that are more effective and more efficient. Sherman (2013), the leading proponent of EBP, is clear that the development of the 'triple-T' (targeting, testing and tracking police activity) amounts to a fundamental shift from reactive and responsive policing and in that sense can be considered a mode for 'controlling the constable'. In terms of Romzek and Dubnick's (1987) four-way typology, they are internal mechanisms that offer low-levels of formal control since they extend the autonomy of officers to develop practice, but in accordance with a core framework of professional expertise. While external agencies are engaged, since scientific researchers and technologists develop the knowledge base, police agencies lead in terms of identifying problems, commissioning research, testing and evaluating outcomes and disseminating professional practice.

The scope for scientific research to enhance police work is clear, and it is apparent that historically there has been a lack of such approaches to policing that has tended to be delivered on the basis of custom and tradition: craft rather than profession. Although harnessing data and research can enable the better identification of crime hot spots and more accurate profiling of individuals at risk of offending and victimisation, and can inform target hardening and crime prevention, concerns about accountability and governance are significant. Historically, in the UK and in the US strategies to enhance police professionalism have been in tension with principles of community policing. Essentially this becomes a debate about the extent to which policing should be subservient to the demands of the public in circumstances where the priorities of the community are in conflict with scientific evidence on effective practice. Police leaders and those who govern them have to square the circle in reconciling tensions between community policing and EBP. This highlights a foundational limitation of EBP in the sense that policing is inherently a political process, with social, cultural and economic dimensions that cannot be always subjected to the Sherman's 'triple-T' approach. Even in circumstances where the evidence is strong, there might not be consensus about policing priorities, and so operational responses will be politically charged and contested. The wider politics of policing cannot be resolved through empirical testing, randomised control trials or systematic review.

Big Data policing strategies raise wider concerns about democratic values where they operate in ways that reinforce existing disproportionalities in police work and in other forms of social, economic and political marginalisation. As Ferguson (2017) and Harcourt (2007) have pointed out, the criminal law does not operate impartially or consistently, and the apparent statistical impartiality of big data and actuarial approaches is illusory when based on established patterns of unequal practice. Potentially, such risks can be reduced by not allowing operational practice to be determined by actuarial results and ensuring that there is transparency and accountability in terms of the methods by which big data is captured and processed. In practice, though, this has proven difficult since the provenance of data often is uncertain and software can be closely guarded by private corporations, and is in any case difficult for non-experts to scrutinise. Again, the wider politics of policing means that technological determinism needs to be avoid. Frightening futures of predictive policing in which self-learning algorithms determine who should be targeted, and when, where and how resources ought to be deployed, are likely to be tempered by realities of limited police resources and technical understanding, as well as cultural and political resistance to change.

Further reading

Bullock, K., Fielding, N. and Holdaway, S. (eds) (2019) *Critical Reflections on Evidence-based Policing*, London: Routledge.

Ferguson, A. Guthrie (2017) *The Rise of Big Data Policing: Surveillance, Race and the Future of Law Enforcement*, New York: New York University Press.

Harcourt, B. (2007) *Against Prediction – Profiling, Policing and Punishing in an Actuarial Age*, Chicago: University of Chicago Press.

Sherman, L.W. (2013) 'The Rise of Evidence-based Policing: Targeting, Testing, and Tracking', *Crime and Justice*, 42(1): 377–451.

6

Internal management and leadership

That police officers have considerable discretion inherent to their role is at the centre of much of the sociology of policing, which is broadly focused on understanding insight into the discrepancies between the 'law in books' and the 'law in practice'. It was noted in earlier chapters that the extent and nature of officer discretion are integral to policing since the application of the law to specific circumstances requires interpretation and the exercise of judgement in terms of identifying the preferred solution from the many potential interventions that might be made. Furthermore, as Reiner (2000: 169) argued, the application of the law to its full extent in all circumstances would be impractical, given that resources are always limited. In ethical and political terms too, the use of discretion is desirable and an established operational principle, such as when (as Scarman noted in his 1981 inquiry into the Brixton disorders) the full enforcement of the law would lead to public disorder. For these reasons, discretion is inherent and valuable in police work. The use of discretion is central to Lipsky's (1980) characterisation of police officers as 'street level bureaucrats' exercising power as they make decisions that have significant implications for their fellow citizens. Nonetheless, there are clearly very many circumstances in which the abuse of police discretion occurs, and it is in that context that many of the measures outlined in this chapter have been developed as methods to 'control the constable' (Jefferson and Grimshaw 1984). Whether the exercise of discretion is considered negative abuse or the positive use of leniency, the central concern is that identified by Neyroud and Beckley (2001: 82), who noted that in the US in the 1970s '... the "discovery" of the true extent of police discretion provoked a heated debate about whether police officers were usurping quasi-judicial functions'. If police officers are not applying the law in ways consistent with the intention of law makers then the concern was that democracy was being subverted. To limit that possibility a range of checks on officer discretion exist within police organisation and management systems, intended to ensure that discretion is exercised within appropriate boundaries.

The chapter begins with an analysis of internal management and leadership approaches overtly and formally developed to prevent and respond to malfeasance of various kinds. In this category are disciplinary regulations and procedures, around which modern policing has always been organised, and the more recent strategy to promote ethical practice. The chapter continues by reviewing other developments in police leadership and management that shape officer behaviour but as a secondary outcome to another primary purpose. The example is used of the introduction of positive arrest policies in response to domestic abuse incidents: a strategy intended to improve outcomes for victims and to decrease reoffending but which effectively curtails the discretion that police officers have in terms of how they interpret and apply their powers. Research on the impact of ethics and integrity programmes indicates how these often intend to promote ideal forms of officer behaviour and decision making, and so to delimit unfettered officer discretion. This is a form of accountability. So, too, the promotion of diversity within policing and cultural transformation is (among other things) heralded as a way of enhancing decision making, again a method of shaping officer behaviour. While Waddington (1999: 38) was correct that the elimination of police discretion is 'virtually unimaginable', administrative processes and technologies curtail its boundaries, and the scope of management ability to scrutinise officer behaviour and decision making has increased. These various policies and practices combine the four elements distinguished by Jarvis (2014), who delineated democratic, assurance, learning and resource as inter-related bases for accountability, as outlined in Chapter 2.

Discipline and police behaviour

From the outset, modern policing has been organised as a 'disciplined service', following a military model with a uniformed, hierarchical structure with a rule-based bureaucracy. Other features of the new Metropolitan Police incorporated perceived benefits of militarism, such as the centrality of drill in police training and the billeting of officers in section houses to help maintain discipline (Reith 1948: 32). Previous policing arrangements in the capital, seen to be ineffective in a period of rapid urbanisation and industrialisation, were replaced by bureaucratic regulations that specified officer conduct in close detail. This included that officers were not to sit down while on patrol and were expected to walk the beat for nine hours at a steady rate of two and a half miles per hour (Reith 1948: 32). Unlike other professions, rules governing police officer conduct have always extended into their private lives: officers used to require permission to marry, and were restricted in terms of where they could live. Targets and micro-management, characteristics associated with the New Public

Management of the early 21st century, and discussed later, clearly have older precedents in police organisations. The early rules and regulations were devised to ward off public hostility to the 'new police' and to distinguish them from the previous arrangements that had become controversial in various respects. The promotion of a publicly visible, effective and restrained police force was pursued symbolically through the adoption of a blue uniform (distinct from the red tunics of the military) but also through rules intended to ensure that officers acted with probity and sobriety. Bailey (1981: 48) argued that an early feature of the force was 'inefficiency, indiscipline (notably drunkenness) and a massive turnover of constables' that was so great that within four years of the establishment of the Metropolitan Police only one sixth of the 3,000 original recruits were still in post (Critchley 1978: 54; Reiner 2000: 20).

Disciplinary practices remained an internal matter for police, much like responding to complaints from the public, until relatively recently. A key feature of recent reforms has been the development of significantly more transparency around the application of disciplinary processes and sanctions. Furthermore, since 2017 amendments to the Police Conduct Regulations, officers are allowed to retire, or resign, from the police service even while they face disciplinary action but such proceedings can continue and sanctions can be implemented against them after their departure. Officers who left policing for more than 12 months can be subject to misconduct hearings if the severity of allegations are significant in terms of public confidence in the police. If found at fault then the ex-officer can be placed on the Barred List and it can be recorded that they would have been dismissed from the service, had they not already left. These provisions are a response to public controversy that officers could avoid investigation by resigning, and, in some cases re-applying to join other police services. The Barred List, administered by the College of Policing, means that there is now a central register of ex-officers prohibited from re-employment. This solves a limitation associated with localism in policing England and Wales whereby each of the 43 constabularies operated relatively autonomously in these matters. The development of national standards is also evident in that the College provides guidance on how disciplinary frameworks are operationalised and sets the standards for professional practice against which officer conduct is assessed. More on this aspect of the College's role is reviewed later in this chapter in relation to the Code of Ethics that it has developed as another mode of holding staff to account. The Code outlines the types of behaviour expected by officers and staff relating to Authority,

Respect & Courtesy; Challenging & Reporting Improper Conduct; Confidentiality; Discreditable Conduct; Duties & Responsibilities; Equality & Diversity; Fitness for Duty; Honesty & Integrity; Orders & Instructions; and Use of Force. The connection between the Code of Ethics and disciplinary frameworks is that the ten elements of the Code are stated in the misconduct regulations as the professional standards against which behaviour is measured.

Police continue to manage disciplinary processes internally, a responsibility that the Chapman (2014) inquiry into police misconduct processes argued was both proportionate and had the effect of ensuring that police leaders assumed responsibility for the behaviour and performance of their staff. An early decision in the complex process of responding to concerns about conduct is an assessment of whether an allegation ought to be dismissed on the basis that there is no case to answer, or that it be regarded as a matter of potential misconduct, or, more seriously, as potential gross misconduct. If considered potential misconduct the case can be dealt with by 'management action', or referred to an internal misconduct meeting. To be treated as gross misconduct, the case must be such that dismissal from the service could be an appropriate sanction and this depends on the substance of the allegation as well as the prior history of the member of staff concerned. Such cases are dealt with by a misconduct hearing. Home Office (2017) data shows that 3,945 complaint and conduct cases were received by the 43 forces of England and Wales in the year to end March 2016, 2,101 of which were dealt with at the lowest level of management advice, 1,115 sent to a misconduct meeting and 729 to a hearing.

Reforms to the processes for misconduct hearings have extended transparency since they are normally held in public, and are managed by a three-person panel, only one of whom is a senior police officer. Alongside the officer is an independent non-police layperson, and hearings are chaired by an independent legally qualified chair. Police services are required to publish details of hearings in advance so that the public can attend as observers, and the findings, outcomes and sanctions (where applicable) have to be publicised for 28 days subsequent to proceedings. Some police services exceed these minimum requirements by providing summary data and records of cases over longer periods. As of 2018, such data was available in relation to 17 police services for the whole of 2017 and indicates that they conducted 262 such cases during that year. Since each case can involve multiple individuals and multiple charges, the data in Figure 6.1 extracts some further detail about those involved, the content of charges, and outcomes. The 262 cases involved 283 individuals (the guidance states that where more than one person is cited in a case they should normally be heard together): 73.5 per cent of those were police constables, only 7.4 per cent were police staff, 8.1 per cent were sergeants, and 5.7 per cent were special constables. It is probable that those staff with greater direct contact with the public might be more likely to attract – whether justified or not – complaints about misconduct from the public.

Figure 6.1 indicates the nature of cases that were considered by misconduct hearings in 2017 in the 17 police service areas where data was available. The most common standard breach was 'discreditable conduct', accounting for 27.6 per cent of cases for which data was available. This likely reflects the breadth of the standard: defined as failing to act 'in a manner which does not discredit the police service or undermine public confidence, whether on or off duty'. The guidelines suggest that the actual conduct underpinning the

Figure 6.1: Misconduct charges by professional standard, selected police services, England and Wales, 2017

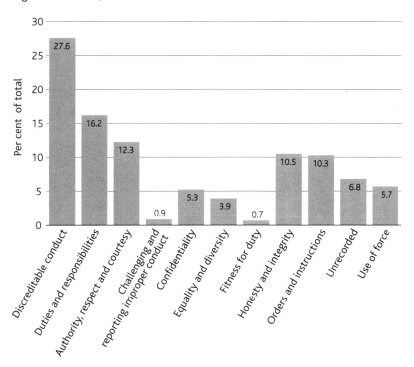

Professional standard

Source: Data derived from 17 police service websites, May 2018

'discrediting' or 'undermining' of public confidence should form the basis of the hearing, rather than the subjective interpretation of the impact the behaviour might have had. A criminal conviction, the guidance notes, would likely amount, in and of itself, to a breach of the standard, whatever the underlying behaviour. While a majority of cases reported on the web involved the alleged breach of just one of the standards, multiple charges were brought in others, such that there were 457 charges across the 262 cases, with one (against two PCs) involving 13 alleged breaches of six of the standards. Reviewing details of the cases suggested that some hearings involved claims that a single action (for example, being convicted of drink driving) led to breaches of more than one standard (for example, 'discreditable conduct' and 'fitness for duty'), whereas others entailed specific charges for different aspects in a course of alleged gross misconduct. As with police crime recording prior to the development of national standards of practice, there is clearly considerable variation in practices, which makes comparative analysis and the identification of trends difficult.

Outcomes of misconduct hearings ranged on a spectrum from 'no case to answer', through 'written warnings', to 'dismissal without notice'. Figure 6.2 indicates that the most common outcome was 'dismissal without notice', reflecting the fact that this outcome is a threshold for determining whether cases allege 'gross misconduct' and so are subject to a hearing rather than resolved at a lower level through a misconduct meeting or management advice. Only 13.3 per cent of cases were 'not proven', with 2.7 per cent leading to the conclusion that there was 'no case to answer', and a further 2.7 per cent 'discontinued'. The data suggests that in nearly eight out of ten cases allegations of misconduct were upheld.

The data presented in the Figures 6.1 and 6.2 and the records of individual hearings were not publicly available until recently, which suggests greater transparency has developed. As in other institutions, the maxim that 'sunlight is the greatest disinfectant' is applied in an effort to enhance public confidence in the police disciplinary process. Nonetheless, provision of the data (beyond the 28-day notice period for individual cases) remains at the discretion of individual police services and in the majority of cases the information is not provided. The spirit of the Chapman (2014) review of police disciplinary process is reflected in the current arrangements, combining local early resolution of 'low-level' cases with greater public transparency around national standards and outcomes. Nonetheless, that police services are not required to present aggregated information from disciplinary processes limits analysis of patterns and trends in the data and identification

Figure 6.2: Misconduct charges by outcome, selected police services, England and Wales, 2017

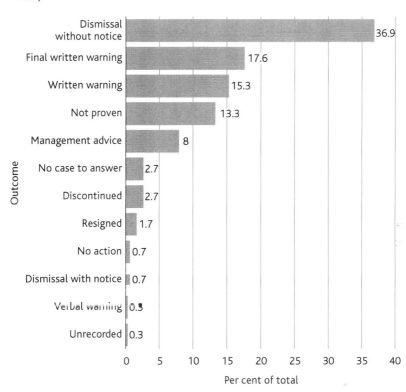

Source: Data derived from 17 police service websites, May 2018

of differences in police services' responses and practices. While the publication of details on individual hearings provides transparency in particular cases, perspectives at the institutional or organisational level cannot be developed in the absence of robust macro–level data.

Ethical policing

The disciplinary frameworks reviewed earlier provide the means to respond retrospectively to officer misconduct. In contrast, ethical codes have developed in many jurisdictions over recent decades with the intention of embedding appropriate behaviour in a more proactive manner. The promotion of police integrity, articulated in a code of ethical behaviour, reflects a wider recognition that police officers and staff operate in complex environments that cannot be captured by prescriptive regulations that prohibit specific actions. Instead, police and staff are expected to meet more generic standards of conduct that encapsulate normative values and ethics consistent with public services more broadly and with prevailing social mores. The precise application of such standards in specific circumstances is a matter for training and leadership within policing and is reinforced by the disciplinary processes that respond to alleged breaches of the codes, as outlined earlier.

In the UK, the College of Policing developed a Code of Ethics, first published in 2013, against a much wider concern about public sector standards arising from the exposure of MPs' financial misconduct, corrupt and illegal media practices, and the inadequate response of the Church, schools and other institutions to child abuse. Some of this wider context is reflected in the Code, in particular in relation to matters of confidentiality of police data, following the Leveson Inquiry's identification of police officers and staff selling information to journalists. Police officer relations with journalists have often and for a long time been a problematic matter in terms of misconduct (Chibnall's [1977] book on media representation of crime and relations with police included a chapter titled 'bloodsoaked cheque books'), and the technological and social changes associated with big data have elevated concerns about probity in this field. Innes (2013) outlined future working practices characterised by 'network enabled policing' based on real-time intelligence and information shaping officers' operational practices. Just as the previous chapter identified accountability challenges at the institutional level, so too big data policing reshapes concerns about ethics and integrity for individual officers and staff (Westmarland and Rowe 2018). Ericson and Haggerty's (1997) study of police data collection, collating, processing, and dissemination led them to characterise officers as 'risk communicators and knowledge brokers' who provided authoritative information about crime and related problems (such as traffic accidents) to a wide range of public and private sector organisations. As the previous chapter noted, the advent of the big data society and the police's privileged access to valuable information makes this a key potential site for misconduct.

Codes of ethics in policing offer a new basis for accountability, reliant on assessing conduct against articulated moral values rather than the more traditional rule-based application of disciplinary regulations. Such approaches have potential important benefits in terms of inculcating a culture of reflexive practice whereby officers and staff are encouraged to recognise that their conduct can have a significant impact on the public that they serve. Another perceived benefit is that a statement of ethical principles can provide a reference point that might encourage officers and staff to address problematic conduct among their colleagues (Rowe and Macauley 2019). In this sense, codes of ethics are intended to promote positive organisational culture and norms that reflect a wider social consensus in relation to police priorities and conduct. Inherently, codes of ethics are aspirational since they promote an ideal model for police officer and staff characteristics, and provide a public statement of expected standards. In this way, codes are adopted in other professions alongside similar guidelines that influence how professional practice is exercised, which is one function of the College of Policing APP standards referred to in the last chapter in relation to the promotion of EBP.

In terms of shaping officer decision making, codes of ethics encourage reflection on how norms and values apply in particular policing situations. As noted, they are aspirational and do not provide any form of blueprint for behaviour. The Code stipulates, for example, that officers and staff will behave in a manner that 'does not bring discredit on the police service or undermine public confidence in policing', a statement that would be difficult to countermand but is problematic in operational terms since it is unclear what might constitute such behaviour. Hough et al (2018) noted that many recent concerns about unethical behaviour among elite leaders have occurred in circumstances in which their actions have been deemed, by the media in many cases, not to chime with the 'public mood'. In such circumstances there is a subjectivity, rather than certainty, about what might constitute misconduct. Not only is there an absence of clear moral objectivity that might underpin statements of ethical behaviour, officers and staff also have to operate according to a multiplicity of guidelines emanating from the various agencies of police governance. The Victim Charter standards, the oath of attestation sworn by all officers, guidelines from PCCs and a plethora of local and national standards (including APP) provide a complex web of guidelines intended to shape conduct and behaviour. While all are legitimate, and there is not necessarily tension or contradiction between them, it remains unclear which is the primary touchstone to which officers and staff should refer. The range of policies and standards operating in policing might explain why research has found that senior officers are sometimes uncertain about details of particular guidelines on officer conduct (Westmarland and Rowe 2018).

Although instances of misconduct are brought against individual or groups of officers, the ethical climate of any organisation has cultural and structural dimensions that shape perceptions of legitimate behaviour. The pressure to get results, which Hough et al (2018) argue underpins some misconduct among senior police leaders, extends to junior ranks and explains some of the 'noble cause corruption' identified in much of the literature (Klockars 1985; Newburn 1999). Furthermore, the 'slippery slope' of police misconduct means that officers' morality shifts incrementally within working relationships with colleagues, which sheds light on how particularly egregious cases of misconduct have often developed within relatively closed specialised squads (Sherman 1985, cited in Newburn 1999). Historical corruption within the West Midlands Serious Crime Squad (Dein 2000) and the Special Demonstration Squad (Lewis and Evans 2013) was sustained in part by a strong internal culture and lack of external scrutiny.

As with other efforts to influence officer and staff behaviour, ethical codes are introduced into a particular cultural and organisational context that will influence the extent and manner in which it is operationalised. The College of Policing produced considerable background material demonstrating how the Code of Ethics was developed in an inclusive manner, and was co-produced and reflects contributions from staff and officers across police services, as well as external partners. No doubt this was to overcome a wider problem evidenced in the research literature that police occupational culture tends to distinguish between the 'codes of the suites' (seen to emanate from remote politicians or police leaders) and the 'codes of the streets' (the formal and informal working practices developed by street-level cops) (Westmarland 2000, 2005). As with many other initiatives intended to reorient police working practices, and as is evident in other organisations, the capacity for 'culture to eat strategy for breakfast' (usually attributed to the management consultant Peter Drucker, see Eaton 2015) is such that codes of ethics risk being weakened by indifference or hostility emanating from working practices. In the UK context, the College of Policing Code of Ethics is strengthened because it explicitly forms the professional standards for disciplinary matters, as outlined in the previous section of this chapter. Unlike other codes introduced in an advisory or voluntary manner, breaches of this Code form the basis for disciplinary action. This enhances the impact of the Code but in ways that move it towards a regulatory approach, thus detracting from efforts to develop a reflexive culture.

A further challenge relating to the cultural context into which the Code is introduced relates to the tenth element that requires officers to challenge or report improper conduct by colleagues. Figure 6.1 shows that less than 1 per cent of misconduct charges in 2017 were brought under this element of the Code of Ethics, which might indicate something of the challenge of developing an organisational culture where concerns about colleagues are raised with management.

As more widely across the public and private sectors, the protection afforded to 'whistle blowers' has been significant in policing, not least because it is often only internal staff members who are aware of misconduct. While formal arrangements can be created to encourage such reporting, it is clear that the 'blue code of silence' that inhibits officers and staff from 'snitching' on colleagues remains a significant challenge (Westmarland and Rowe 2018). The difficulty of auditing professional practice was identified by the Jones (2018) inquiry into high death rates at the Gosport War Memorial Hospital. The inquiry report found that in the absence of effective audit systems, 'whistle blowing' was one of the few ways of raising concerns about clinical decisions, but that staff who acted in this manner faced being 'shunned by colleagues and, in some cases, obliged to emigrate to pursue their career' (Jones 2018: 81). In policing, the cultural pressures not to report misconduct are such that the code of the streets often takes precedence over the more formal Code of Ethics in an environment where loyalty and teamwork are regarded as integral to police work. The 'blue code of silence' (Westmarland 2005) is preserved because officers lack confidence in their management (Huberts et al 2007). In effect, they are worried that they will be blamed, stigmatised (Miller 2003) or ignored, and their information will have no effect on the organisation or the individual's behaviour. Some officers believe that any violations they report may not be investigated and that by pointing an accusatorial finger, whether at individuals or the institution, they may be treated unfairly and without impartially (Kääriäinen et al 2008).

One of the problems identified in this context points to the need to recognise the organisational as well as individual dimensions of police misconduct. While codes of ethics and professional standards are articulated, usually, in terms of the behaviour and conduct expected of individual officers and staff, research suggests that it is a lack of trust in systems to report and investigate misconduct that inhibits whistle blowers. Studies have shown that the problem of non-reporting of unethical or corrupt behaviour lies with organisational systems (Newburn 1999; Chan 2003; Punch 2009). In circumstances where misconduct is suspected, colleagues are reluctant to report concerns because they feel that effective action is unlikely to be forthcoming and that, with little to gain, the risk of being exposed by systems that cannot be relied on to preserve anonymity is too great to make reporting viable (Westmarland 2013). Organisational dimensions are also significant since senior officers might not always be aware of detailed policy provisions relating to professional conduct, and so might be reluctant informally to challenge behaviour that might be inappropriate (Westmarland and Rowe 2018). Some police services have sought to overcome the reluctance to report by introducing anonymous phone or web facilities for officers and staff to pass on concerns, but the disciplinary value of such information is limited since further investigation may be difficult without an identified complainant. Another strategy has been to introduce campaigns designed to reverse the cultural opposition to reporting concerns about colleagues' behaviour, such as the 'Speak Up' programme introduced in New Zealand Police (Rowe and Macauley, 2019). Other management systems such as early warning indicators can be used to identify officers and staff who might be 'at risk' of misconduct on the basis of their more general workplace performance, for example, high absence rates or concerns about welfare. 'Big data' approaches such as those outlined in Chapter 5 might be applied to identify patterns of behaviour that are not in themselves problematic but that might be correlated with misconduct. If patterns of police conduct that might be legitimate, such as carrying out above-average numbers of stops and searches are correlated with illegitimate behaviour then there is the potential for services to identify officers and other staff more likely to breach ethical and disciplinary standards. All the caveats identified in Chapter 5 (including those relating to the reliability and ethics of big data strategies) apply in this context just as in policing more widely.

Management as micro-governance

Just as employee support and assistance programmes can be used by police services to identify potential disciplinary issues, so, too, wider management and organisational practices provide internal means to hold officers to account and to shape the way in which discretion is exercised. As McLaughlin et al (2001) noted, the application of techniques of New Public Management to policing in the UK from the 1990s, as elsewhere in the public sector, was intended to promote efficiency, effectiveness and accountability in financial terms. Through the introduction of performance indicators and targets, police leaders and those with local and national governance responsibility were able to compare performance between Basic Command Units (BCUs) and police services, who were grouped into 'families' so that comparison was between forces with similar characteristics. These 'hard' forms of accountability, carried out by the governing agencies examined in Chapter 3, embedded models of management and organisation that were new to policing. The measurement, at police service level, of performance relating to sanctioned detections, for example, was disaggregated down to BCU, beat team and the level of individual officers, whose working practices were measured and scrutinised in ways not previously applied to policing. These techniques were enabled by the interrelated development of clearer national standards in terms of what was to be counted and in what manner, and system and technological changes designed to facilitate this. Requiring officers to report their working practices in a micro-managed way developed as a means of governance at a distance, through the creation of quasi-market indicators that would reveal patterns of effective and ineffective performance. These new forms of accountability in policing have replaced longer-established command and control approaches (as outlined in earlier chapters) with 'at-a-distance' governance through self-regulation whereby internal management processes provide opportunities for micro-governance (Chan 1999).

These techno-political innovations have contributed to the development of police management systems and mentalities that have considerably expanded the capability of supervisory staff to oversee and interrogate the actions of frontline officers. Modalities and technologies of police leadership and management can be considered 'soft' forms of accountability in the sense that while they are not formally presented as governance mechanisms to regulate officer behaviour, they nonetheless bear influence in such terms. The relative invisibility of police decision making has long been regarded as a key feature of officer discretion, as was examined in Chapter 2. The capability of shift sergeants, inspectors and chief officers to scrutinise the behaviour and decision making of constables engaged in patrol work that was largely unstructured has been limited during much of the period since the introduction of the 'modern' police. The two-way radio and Unit Beat Policing introduced in Britain in the 1960s (Brain 2000) expanded the capacity of supervisors to scrutinise officer behaviour, but more recent technological change (coupled with political imperatives such as those outlined later) have rapidly increased the 'reach' of internal managerial accountability. Through the introduction of PACE (Police and Criminal Evidence Act 1984) Codes of Conduct to 21st-century 'phablets' (an amalgam of smart phone and tablet), with GIS capacity to identify officer whereabouts, and BWCs (Dymond and Hickman 2017) the surveillance powers to which officers are subjected have greatly expanded.

The technological panoptical powers applied to officers, and the likely behavioural adjustments to which they give rise, are coupled with managerial processes in terms of required conduct. While codes of practice and standards of APP provide relatively high-level guidelines to behaviour in particular circumstances, other requirements more directly curtail discretion by forcing specific actions in determined situations. New forms of micro-governance have developed, enabling supervisory officers to exercise 'on-the-spot accountability', as described by the College of Policing. Many of the managerial processes of this kind have been developed in order to curtail the exercise of police officer discretion in ways identified as incompatible with prevailing social norms and standards identified by governance bodies. For example, positive or mandatory arrest policies in cases of domestic abuse have been introduced partly on the basis of evidence purporting to show that such interventions reduce repeat offending (Sherman et al 1992) and also to prevent officers from 'no criming' such offences because they regard them as troublesome and 'weary' policing problems and so seek to opt out of conducting an investigation (Baldry and Sebire 2016). Often the arrest policies, which require an officer to arrest the suspected perpetrator (rather than opt for another course of action), have been coupled with a risk assessment process that requires officers to complete a survey with victims such that there is then capacity to identify those for whom there is the greatest prospect of the abuse recurring and escalating (Grant and Rowe 2011). In a political and social environment where the problem of domestic abuse is more widely recognised as a priority and in which there is a strong consensus that police and criminal justice responses have been poor, risk management and crime recording processes combine to delimit officer discretion and are forms of micro-governance.

Similarly, in another area where policing has widely been identified as inadequate, responses of hate crime require officers to 'flag' incidents by selecting a particular database field when entering details of cases into computer systems. Cases marked are automatically forwarded to supervisory officers, who are then required to ensure that policies on victim support and the conduct of investigations are properly adhered to. As Ericson and Haggerty (1997) demonstrated, the administrative requirements of case-handling systems actively shape officer behaviour – since certain information has to be collected, priorities are shaped and officer time allocated to that rather than other dimensions of an investigation. Moreover, they argued that the information demands of administrative systems also shape how officers conceptualise crime problems; indeed this is precisely the purpose of the requirements identified earlier in relation to domestic abuse investigations, hate crime and so forth. Ericson and Haggerty (1997) argued that the bureaucratic and administrative requirements placed on officers and staff are not just retrospective means of collating and storing data but play a proactive role in shaping how the police role is understood and performed. They state (1997: 33):

> Police work is … prospectively structured by the categories and classifications of risk communication and by the technologies for communicating knowledge internally and externally. The communication formats provide the means through which the police think, act and justify their actions. These formats are in turn structured by the expert knowledge of risk required by police managers and external institutions.

The shaping of the ways in which police 'think, act and justify' their practice commences, often, from the initial point of contact members of the public have with control room staff, who are primarily civilians responsible for logging information and dispatching officers to jobs. Integral to this process is the grading of incidents in terms of the priority of the response required and 'flagging' an incident that might be a hate crime or domestic abuse, or have other features that mean urgent action is deemed necessary. Lumsden and Black (2018) cite Manning's (1982) observation that the role of the call-handling staff is to act as a 'screen or a mesh' through which diverse and sometimes incoherent accounts from the public are sorted into those that are 'police relevant' and then allocating them to operational staff. Logging a report in police IT systems as an incident of domestic abuse, for example, impacts on the actions of police as they arrive at the scene and influences the likely outcomes in circumstances where officers are aware that their actions are monitored by the line managers. To avoid 'in-the-job trouble' (Young 1991) officers might act in ways that comply with formal requirements even when these contradict their professional judgement of the circumstances of particular cases (Rowe 2007).

In such ways, modalities and techniques of case investigation and line management practices directly and indirectly shape officer behaviour and restrict the repertoire of responses available to officers. The intention of this micro-governance is to ensure that police responses reflect the standards established by law and policy but in curtailing officer discretion, sometimes very drastically, it threatens to de-skill officers and remove their scope for professional judgement. The contradictions between such modes of micro-governance and wider promotion of the notion that officers act with professional independence and judgement remain largely under-explored. One exception to this was Chan's work in New South Wales, which found that the bureaucratic measures developed to promote better scrutiny of officer behaviour in the 1990s resulted in lower morale, cynicism, heavier administrative burdens and a defensive 'tick box' management style (Chan 2003).

Despite concerns about the impact of management systems on the professional exercise of police discretion, the capacity of officers and staff to resist or circumvent the micro-government of their behaviour should not be underestimated. In the case of the 'requirement' for officers to complete risk assessment with domestic abuse survivors, for example, officers have been able to manipulate their working practices to complete tasks on their own terms (Grant and Rowe 2011). The use of BWCs might be a technology for the surveillance of officer conduct, as well as their expressed primary purpose of evidence gathering, but officers continue to decide when and where the cameras are activated. The requirement for officers to issue receipts to individuals subject to stop and search might be intended to allow monitoring for bias and over-use (among other purposes) but officers' decisions not to stop and search an individual (which might also be a form of misconduct and bias) cannot be captured by this form of oversight. Since discretion is an inevitable, and – when exercised appropriately – a positive feature of police work, the capacity of management systems and technology to curtail it is limited. Nonetheless the surveillance capabilities of supervisory officers to track officer activity and to ensure compliance with operational standards has been expanded as, for example, GIS and portable technology is ubiquitous in police work as elsewhere.

Conclusion

If police accountability is understood – as Jefferson and Grimshaw (1984) suggested that it should be – as the means to ensure that police officers act in accordance with prevailing policies, laws and normative standards, then it is clear that many internal management processes should be considered in these terms. Three broad and overlapping sets of strategies have been identified. A military-style command and control model of discipline was established as the 'new police' developed in Britain from 1829 through to the middle of that century, and is evident in many police services globally. That policing is a 'disciplined' service has various connotations in terms of a hierarchical, regulated and command-based organisation, including the application of rules and regulations that govern officer behaviour. As with the administration of complaints from the public, the application of disciplinary procedures remained a largely internal and private matter for constabularies until relatively recently. The increasing transparency of police disciplinary processes in recent years, primarily through the provision of access to hearings and the publication of proceedings on police service websites, has been consistent with other public sector organisations. Nonetheless, the control and management of such processes remains with police leaders, who retain significant discretionary powers in terms of how allegations of misconduct are treated. The Chapman Inquiry (2014), which has shaped recent reforms of disciplinary processes in policing, suggested that police leaders ought to retain this central role in order to retain responsibility for staff conduct, and to increase the potential to develop organisational learning. The provision of information in terms of gross misconduct hearings that are held in public provides opportunities for public scrutiny but the data presented earlier indicates that this is collated and published inconsistently across forces in ways that make the identification of trends and patterns problematic.

Another logic of governing officer conduct is provided by the development of codes of ethics and integrity programmes designed not, as with disciplinary regulations, for the prohibition of unacceptable behaviour, but for the promotion of aspirational standards. In Britain, the Code of Ethics developed by the College of Policing in 2013 is linked to disciplinary processes since the ten professional standards it promotes form the benchmark against which conduct is judged. Codes of ethics can provide a framework for professional behaviour and can be used to develop a more inclusive, diverse and reflexive internal culture (Rowe and Macauley 2019). Organisational theory suggests that codes and narratives form 'espoused values' and are an important part of culture, along with artefacts and underlying assumptions, tacit knowledge and implicit beliefs about roles and duties (Schein 2010). Kaptein (2008) demonstrates that 'discussability', the capacity to share narratives openly, is a key component of ethical culture. Kaptein (2011) further found that reflective cultures are closely aligned with positive experiences in people speaking up in organisations. In these ways, codes of ethics can provide significant statements and opportunities for reflexive practice and can encourage challenges to unacceptable behaviour. In the policing context, the potential for codes to lead to organisational change is likely to be hampered by cultural imperatives towards group loyalty and the resulting 'blue code of silence', coupled with suspicion of codes perceived to be remote from frontline police experiences.

Further reading

Hough, M., May, T., Hales, G. and Belur, J. (2018) 'Misconduct by Police Leaders in England and Wales: an Exploratory Study', *Policing and Society*, 28: 541–52.

Ramshaw, P., Silvestri, M. and Simpson, M. (eds) (2019) *Police Leadership: Changing Landscapes*, London: Palgrave.

Westmarland, L. and Rowe, M. (2016) 'Police Ethics and Integrity: Can a New Code Overturn the Blue Code?', *Policing and Society: An International Journal of Research and Policy*, DOI: 10.1080/10439463.2016.1262365.

7

Transparency and the external gaze

Previous chapters have considered mechanisms and principles of police governance in terms of the various formal institutions and policies introduced to hold police to account. Some of these have been explicitly developed for such purposes and are primarily responsible for the direction and oversight of police services. They are rule based, legally constituted and bureaucratic. PCCs and HMICFRS are principal actors in this regard. Other agencies and practices guide and shape police officer discretion (and so provide some measure of governance) in more indirect ways, as a supplement to other functions. Chapter 6 analysed the role of technology, such as BWCs, and policy requirements, such as positive arrest policies in relation to domestic abuse, that effectively shape officer behaviour (and so are a form of governance) even though this might not be their principal or primary function. Returning to Romzek and Dubnick's (1987) four-way model of accountability, which distinguished between internal and external sources with either high or low degrees of control, the discussion has focused on external and internal mechanisms with high levels of control expressed in legal and bureaucratic forms. The book has also examined various types of professional forms of accountability that are also internally sourced, such as complaints and discipline, and the development of professional standards.

In contrast, the focus in this chapter is instead predominantly on external forms of oversight that offer low levels of control, at least in formal legal terms. Similar arrangements were described by White (2016) in the context of the British private security industry as forms of 'soft accountability'. In his analysis of the debacle surrounding the role of private security in policing the 2012 London Olympics, White noted that media scrutiny, public opinion and political pressure combined to place considerable opprobrium on the company G4S as it became apparent that it would be unable effectively to fulfil its contract to provide security for the games. Media exposés of ill-trained and poorly resourced staff and potential security risks, and the resulting need for police and armed forces to be drafted in to fill the gaps in provision, contributed to significant fines being levied on G4S, along with reputational damage. The nature of 'soft' accountability in relation to policing is explored later, with a particular focus on the impact of 'citizen journalism' and critical analysis of the capacity of technology as a form of regulation in a sousveillance society. Power and authority, in formal terms, are diffuse and transient in such practices. Many of the other, more formal, mechanisms of police accountability analysed in earlier chapters have sought to increase the transparency of police work. Increasing the reporting requirements around stop and search, for example, or publication online of misconduct cases, are efforts to expose previously hidden activities such that citizens have greater capacity to scrutinise those in power. Similar principles underlie the recording and broadcasting via social media of police practices as illustrated in the discussion that follows. A crucial difference, however, is that in the context of external 'soft' accountability, transparency is enhanced beyond the control of police, government and the state. This shift in surveillant power – from the central panoptical state to private citizens – is integral to the concept of sousveillance and related claims that technological developments expand democracy and accountability. Mann and Ferenbok (2013: 27) link technological change to social and political accountability as follows:

> In recent years … mobile networked devices have been combined with social networks that can trigger political disruption and change. Coupling portability, capture, storage and distribution, portable media has allowed us to bring along content, but mobile media (portable media with dedicated internet infrastructures) provides significant opportunities for individuals not only to capture records of abuse of power or corruption, but also to quickly distribute and communicate it to others for political action.

In charting the growing capacity for recording and mediating the actions of the powerful by the powerless, Mann and Ferenbok (2013) argue that analysis should move beyond consideration of 'surveillance' and 'sousveillance' (the former being the actions of the powerful and the latter the actions of the powerless). To this end they apply a framework of 'veillance' (or 'equiveillance') since there is increasing parity between state and citizen in an era of mutual and multiple observation. While power differentials still shape such relations, they are fluid, relative to other forms of oversight, and unpredictable. Many of those claims are critically analysed later in this chapter, after an outline of these emerging forms of 'soft' accountability – termed by Goldsmith (2010) as the 'new accountability' – is provided.

A picture is worth a thousand words?

From the 1980s onwards there has been what has been labelled a 'visual turn' within social science research (Pauwels 2000), as evidenced by an expansion in visual sociology (Harper 1988) and visual criminology (Carrabine 2012). Closely tied in with a theoretical focus on the communicative, social and political power of visual imagery has been the expansion of social media and camera phone technology such that individuals have unprecedented opportunities to capture and publish images. The democratic potential of social media was much heralded during the so-called 'Arab Spring' from 2011, during which popular uprisings against authoritarian regimes including those in Tunisia, Libya, Syria and Iran were coordinated by citizens enabled by social media to organise protest and political opposition in ways previously not possible. Howard and Hussain (2013) analysed the onset and development of the popular uprisings in terms of whether the role of digital technology and social media amounts to a 'fourth wave' of democracy. While they noted that the impact of the Arab Spring, in terms of creating sustained democratic reform, remains questionable, and is likely to vary from country to country, the capacity of citizens to change society using social media suggests powerful new paths for liberation and democracy. Similarly, the development of the anti-capitalist protest movements in Wall Street, in London and elsewhere – the Occupy protests – were virtual digital campaigns, as much as they were physical protests against the 1 per cent global elite identified as controlling global wealth. In addition to using social media as a central platform for their activity the Occupy movement continued practices of surveillance of police activity that emerged around the Cop Watch strategy developed by environmental protestors, among others, from the 1990s onwards. In direct response to police surveillance, protestors against road-building programmes, various G8/9 summit meetings, animal testing, fox hunting, and such like, began filming police operations and sharing details of officers and tactics on websites so that counter-intelligence, gathered, processed and distributed by citizens against the state, could further resistance through enhancing oversight and scrutiny of the powerful.

In terms of their use of photography, a three-fold typography of contemporary protest can be identified: first, use by protests and campaigns of visual images as a general technique to garner publicity and support; second, the use of photographs to challenge dominant media discourse; and, third, the use of photography for forensic purposes to challenge policing, security and legal malpractice. Ferrell et al (2008: 184) expressed the growing development of a visual criminology in the following terms:

> The everyday experience of late modernity may or may not be suffused with crime, but it is certainly suffused with images, and with images of crime. Television offers an avalanche of crime imagery, from local news reports to prime-time crime dramas ... Criminals videotape their crimes, protesters photograph their protests, police shoot far more images than they do people, security agents scrutinize the image-making of criminals and protesters – and a million surveillance monitors keep pace.

The images collected by citizen journalists might also serve the third category in this typology of counterveillance protest photography: those activities that seek to challenge legal, policing and security malpractices. The range of types of resistance to surveillance is broad: from individual efforts to conceal identity to more organised political challenges, some of which might emanate from oversight groups with institutional power (Marx 2009). The focus here is not on resistance per se, but rather the ways in which individuals and groups have sought to use the techniques and technologies of surveillance to challenge and subvert state practices. The ubiquity of photography at public order events is readily apparent, not least from visual records themselves, which tend to depict diverse amateur and professional photographers (including police staff) as well as protestors and other participants. Notably, amateur photographs have captured significant incidents in recent public order protest events, such as the beating of Ian Tomlinson during the London G20 protests in 2009, a case returned to later in this chapter. The apparent authenticity of such grassroots images makes them compelling in an era when reality television has become a significant genre in the depiction of crime and the 'unmasking' of police deviance. The undercover images of police recruits engaging in racist banter in training school, as shown on the influential 2003 documentary *The Secret Policeman*, matched in terms of style and format earlier covert footage of the alleged killers of Stephen Lawrence as they enacted their fantasies of racist violence (Rowe 2004). In addition to the informal participation of witnesses capturing images of police or private security malfeasance at protest sites have been the activities of relatively organised groups who seek to uncover and so to challenge state surveillance. Amid concerns about police use of surveillance photography to suppress civil liberties and intimidate protestors, loosely organised groups of protestors, journalists and campaigners instigated their own databases collating information about police monitoring. This was in response to the use of surveillance by police against protestors and journalists as a form of harassment and intimidation that apparently sought to inhibit civil liberties and democratic protest, and became part of the 'spy policing' model exposed in Britain in the early 21st century and leading to the establishment of the Pitchford Inquiry in 2015 (Evans and Lewis 2013; Marshall and Thomas 2017; Schlembach 2018). Following intensive police intelligence gathering around various Climate Camp protests in the period since 2007, the Fitwatch network was established to resist police tactics against protestors, provide advice to those subject to police attention and to make public information about police officers and operations that were themselves based on surveillance conducted by Forward Intelligence Teams (FITs).

The Fitwatch website included details and photographs of named and numbered police officers, particular operations, police units, and advice on legal matters and related subjects, such as 'stop and search', and the use of the Regulation of Investigatory Powers Act and so on. Information was collated on the site in a format that mirrors state and police databases and, although of limited scale, allowed for searches and cross-referencing. In keeping with similar organisations, such as Statewatch, Fitwatch provided a general critique of the extent of police surveillance gathering and sought to enhance accountability and democratic oversight by developing a counterweight to the surveillant power of the state. The activities of Fitwatch were heavily criticised by police, and legal action succeeded in forcing the closure of the website. Mann and Ferenbok (2013: 31) suggest such responses demonstrate that 'Police … [do] not respond well to being photographed in public while they were supposedly working for the public. Is it somehow these authoritarians understand that sousveillance represents not only a challenge to its intuitional gaze, but also as a limit of the power of surveillance?'

The extent to which the powerful seek to use the law to restrict scrutiny of their own actions, as in the Fitwatch case (or the G20 summit protests in Toronto that Mann and Ferenbok [2013] cite), also demonstrates, however, that there remain significant power differentials. Even where those conducting veillance on police have a degree of equivalence in terms of the technological capacity and ability to broadcast material to the public, it is evident that police have more considerable power in terms of resources and knowledge, and culturally. The 'equiveillance' that Mann and Ferenbok (2013) identify seems to be some way distant in terms of policing, even though social media has played an important role in exposing misconduct in some cases. Since the financial, political and cultural capital available to some groups experiencing police attention clearly is not commensurate with that of law enforcement agencies then the capacity to use technology as a means to enhance governance or extended democratic oversight seems limited. While it might be that there are more photographic records of police malfeasance than used to be the case, it is far from clear that these have necessarily led to greater accountability. The 'new accountability' Goldsmith (2010) outlined might enable greater communicative reach in ways that are difficult for authorities to control or regulate, but this does not inevitably mean that grievances are more effectively addressed in political or legal terms. Some of the contextual factors that influence the impact of social media oversight of police action are outlined in the following discussion.

The power of an image: recognising the importance of context

The democratic capacity of photography to expose abuse of power cannot be taken for granted and is dependent on a host of wider factors relating to context and circumstances of the activists and events and the political and social milieu that they occupy. A simple 'problem-response' model such that the visual capture and identification of abuse of power secures justice and reform needs to be empirically tested. This is a significant limitation in terms of Mann and Ferenbok's (2013) analysis, which is conceptually important but pays no attention to the processes by which corruption and abuse of power – even when identified by processes of sousveillance – may become subject to processes of governance such that individuals are held to account and institutional practices reformed. Moreover, the capacity of sousveillance to monitor police is constrained by the capacity of individual officers, and police organisations, to resist efforts of protestors to monitor their activity. In addition to legal measures such as those that closed the Fitwatch website, Waghorn (2016) identifies a range of physical and technological measures police have used to thwart the use of drones by protestors seeking to surveil operations at protest sites. In addition to electronic countermeasures to disable drones, for example by disrupting GPS, police have shot drones from the sky and officers have obscured their identification numbers such that it is more difficult to identify particular individuals (Waghorn 2016). While it is important to examine officers' capacity to resist surveillance – both externally from the public and internally from within police organisations – it must also be noted that not all officers in all circumstances regard such recordings negatively. Just as Newburn and Hayman (2002) found that police perceived benefits that had arisen from the use of CCTV recording within police stations, so, too, Sandhu (2017) argued that officers identified value from the video and recording of their actions in terms of crime control and image management. The capacity of police themselves to produce their own social media content and to participate in discussion of other footage on social media platforms means that they are not simply passive actors being recorded by other parties but are active agents able to contest narratives of particular representations that purport to show misconduct. For these and related reasons, Sandhu's (2017: 4) study of police responses to cameras in a Canadian city led him to note that: 'the police have a conflicted relationship with cameras which sometimes includes a desire to avoid being recorded, but often includes a desire to adopt cameras to produce and share imagery that offers a favourable depiction of the police'.

Despite efforts to conceal their identity, various cases illustrate the capacity of 'citizen journalists' to capture images that identify officer malpractice. One of the earliest such examples was the recording, by a passing motorist, of the beating of Rodney King by officers from Los Angeles Police Department (LAPD) in 1992. The officers were identified and prosecuted, as is discussed later, and as was the case in many of the other instances of police violence associated with the Black Lives Matter movement in the US and elsewhere (Richardson 2017), video and photographic images have identified officers involved. The dramatic power of visual images secured by members of the public was clearly demonstrated in the police assault on Ian Tomlinson during the protests against the G8 summit held in London in 2009. Video footage captured by a bystander showed Tomlinson walk through and in front of a line of police officers in riot gear, one of whom pushed him in the back causing him to fall, face first, onto the pavement. A few minutes later, having walked away from the scene, Tomlinson collapsed and died of an apparent heart attack. In many respects this episode – along with video footage taken one day later that purported to show a protestor, Nicola Fisher, being beaten on the legs by an officer – epitomised the counterveillant potential of photography in contemporary public disorder. Rituals of denial that have emanated from police in previous cases in which assaults have been alleged were not apparent in these more recent cases. As the anniversary of Tomlinson's death arrived, an internal Metropolitan Police report into the death of Blair Peach at an Anti-Nazi League demonstration in London in 1979 was made public. The report upheld long-standing claims that Peach had been struck by a police officer. Unlike in the cases of Tomlinson and Fisher, no photographic evidence existed in relation to the events that befell Peach and the identity of the officer who struck him remains unknown. In the cases of Tomlinson and Fisher, in the age of social media, the officers involved in the two incidents were quickly identified and legal proceedings were taken against both. To this extent the capacity of sousveillance to hold officers to account is enhanced by citizen journalists and new media environments, which disrupt traditional media 'hierarchies of power' (Becker 1967, cited in Greer and McLaughlin 2010) that reflect the dominant news agendas of elite groups and focus on protestor rather than police violence.

The broader politics of recording and broadcasting incidents of police violence in various cases associated with the US Black Lives Matter movement in recent years are analysed by Richardson (2017), who makes a similar argument that technology has helped to challenge dominant narratives of violence. She notes that Black Twitter has become an important public space in which footage of police violence and subsequent protests are represented as part of an historical pattern of civil rights abuses and linked to other human rights abuses. Richardson (2017) argued that the politics of witnessing, associated, for example, with Jewish commemoration of the Shoah, has been transformed by social media since remote witnessing is made possible as citizens watch (sometimes in a livestreaming format) events previously hidden. She outlines these new means of bearing witness (Richardson 2017: 677):

> The crisis of witnessing is an apt frame through which to study the outpouring of black citizen journalism in Ferguson and Baltimore too. In the Jewish tradition of witnessing, survivors speak to commemorate the slain, and to verify that atrocities indeed transpired. In doing so, witnesses help create a long, thematic thread of narrative that links similar human rights violations to one another throughout history, rather than regarding each new violation as an isolated incident. Just as the modern persecution of the Jews almost always reflects on the Holocaust, modern black witnessing carries the spirit of the US Civil Rights Movement, which peaked during the 1960s. When African American distant witnesses in Ferguson took to the streets to protest the murder of Michael Brown, for example, they used mobile

devices and social media to circulate familiar visual tropes
that are associated with Dr. Martin Luther King.

Challenging dominant media and political narratives, as noted in
relation to the Arab Spring in the earlier discussion, is a central feature
of social media, technology and the citizen journalist. In these broad
social media content can be significant in terms of police governance
and accountability. They can counter powerful representations of
political conflict and shape public debate in relation to the normative
standards applied to policing – what is justice, what is fair policing,
what is proportionate use of violence? Social media footage can shape
perceptions of police legitimacy and helps inform the underlying
framework against which police behaviour is evaluated. Further to
Loader and Mulcahy's (2001a, 2001b) analysis of the capacity of police
to 'legitimately name' (and diagnose) social problems and that such an
agenda setting is an important component of power, perhaps social
media representation of police malpractice provides counterbalance.
This has at least the potential to shape the governance of policing. It
was noted in Chapter 6 that ethical codes of police conduct provide
broad standards to which officers are held to account but do not tend
to specify detailed guidelines for operational behaviour. For example,
the College of Policing Code of Ethics states that officers will use
force in ways that 'are necessary, proportionate and reasonable in all
the circumstances', the interpretation of which will be done in social,
cultural and political contexts shaped by new forms of media. This
extends the more situational practices identified by Waghorn (2016),
who noted that police officers' behaviour at protest sites was self-
modified in anticipation that they were being subject to surveillance
by drones flown by protestors, illustrating in the 21st century the
panoptical power of Bentham's prison design.
   Clearly a form of visual determinism needs to be avoided in
consideration of the counterveillance potential of photography in
protest situations. One reason for caution is that even stark visual
representation of police use of violence, for example, requires
interpretation and is likely to be judged differently among diverse
audiences. The use of violence, in particular, is complex in terms of
exposés of police behaviour since the delivery of force by an officer
is not inherently problematic; the context in which violence is used
might be such that the action was necessary and legitimate. Such
wider context is often difficult to discern in a video clip, which
might capture the immediate action but not the preceding interaction
or the broader environment. In such circumstances, images require

interpretation and this will inevitably lead to different perspectives among audiences. In their analysis of online commentary further to the posting on YouTube of footage of the fatal police shooting of Oscar Grant at a Californian subway station, Antony and Thomas (2010) found not only diversity of opinion in terms of the more appropriate political and protest response, but also considerable debate about the ethics of posting the footage in the first instance. Similarly, Reilly (2015) charted that social media footage of 'anti-Tesco riots' in Bristol in 2011 were interpreted by audiences in very different ways such that condemnation of police use of force from some quarters was matched by calls from others for the police to use still greater force in response to protestors. Moreover, as many examples illustrate, documentary footage of malpractice tends to reproduce a model of organisational deviance that presents problems in terms of individual culpability of an officer and sidelines policy or organisational factors. The wrongdoing that is exposed is couched in terms of individual officers who use force indiscriminately, for example, and Edwards (2009: 453) argued that this was a central feature of the documentary photograph 'that employs a rhetoric of individualization – translating social situations into individual tragedies'. While this might encourage the viewer to reconsider 'the mob' and can expose police violence, it does so in a framework that reproduces established folk devils of individualised police deviance – familiar from popular culture as well as news media exposés – but reveals nothing of cultural, institutional and policy factors that shape operational policing.

Another concern relates to the danger of simplifying conceptualisation of the monitoring of police and state behaviour, as though that role can only be fulfilled by protest groups or independent monitors. While it may be, as Mawby (2009), for example, argued, that criminal justice agencies are among the most watched in late modern society, it should not be assumed that they are only viewed through external or critical lenses. Photography and video technology have been widely used for surveillance and monitoring of police officers for several decades, for example the use of CCTV recording in custody suites (Newburn and Hayman 2002). These technologies may have had additional remits, in terms of evidence gathering and crime scene analysis, and they might not have been wholly effective in terms of prevention of malpractice, but forms of internal surveillance have been developed by the very agencies subject to the gaze of protestor cameras. Moreover, the use of visual images by police and other agencies, such as the court service, should not be constructed only in negative terms as an encroachment on civil liberties or personal privacy: the use of video evidence to collect and present statements from vulnerable witnesses in courts has become a familiar practice, for example, and one that might reduce the traumatisation of crime victims by the legal system.

A third set of concerns, and consequently questions for further research, relates to the audiences that view images captured and distributed by protestors, bystanders and citizen journalists, as mentioned earlier. Just as media research in general, and that into crime in particular, for a long time paid only scant attention to audience effects, so, too, consideration of the impact of images of police and private security malpractice tends to assume an audience reaction that might not actually be forthcoming. Responses to visual representations are likely to be contingent on a host of demographic, situational and social factors such that audience reactions may not correspond to intentions of photographers and campaigners, or the interpretations of academic and critical viewers. This matter is returned to later in the discussion.

A fourth concern in relation to the nature of contemporary veillance is that the data captured and broadcast on social media platforms – material that is likely to include images of members of the public, offenders and protestors, as well as police officers – is likely to become part of the mesh that feeds the big data policing critiqued in Chapter 5. Content that is publicly available on social media platforms can form a resource for scrutiny and accountability of police behaviour while, at the same time, forming a source of intelligence to inform future policing operations. In an environment where there is increasing equality in terms of the surveillant powers of the state and of citizens then material collected by both parties can be utilised in both directions: both to enhance oversight of police actions and, in circumstances where members of the public are also visually captured by smart phones, drones or private CCTV, to further extend the capacity of big data policing.

The developing parity of surveillant capacity between powerful agents of the state and hitherto subordinate citizens is further illustrated in relation to the use by police of BWCs, as mentioned earlier. Ariel et al (2017) argued that the significant (almost 100 per cent) reduction in citizen complaints that they measured in sites where officers used BWCs is partly explained by the 'contagious accountability' that develops in circumstances where officers anticipate that their interactions with the public are being observed. The impact of BWCs is on officers and citizens alike as all parties' demeanour and behaviour unfolds in anticipation that they are being videoed.

As Waghorn (2016) noted, and as was discussed earlier, officers modify their actions in expectation that they are being recorded by drones. Ariel et al (2017) suggest similar behavioural responses to BWCs but that these are compounded by concurrent expectation that encounters with citizens are being recorded by smart phone and related technology operated by bystanders. This suggests that networks of surveillance, incorporating systems operated by those in both superordinate and subordinate positions, interact to develop forms of oversight and accountability that need to be understood in collective terms. It is the combined effect of different forms of monitoring that shape police–public interactions.

The importance of the audience

In terms of the limitations of social media as a means for democratic accountability, it is worth noting that Bruns et al's (2013) analysis of Twitter use during the uprisings in Libya, Egypt and elsewhere suggests caution. They distinguish different types of behaviour among users and so indicate that regarding 'social media' as a singular form is misleading. They note that some content surrounding the Arab Spring was reactive reporting of events, and not all was tied to any coherent programme for change. Furthermore, the distinction between new and old media was blurred since some content recirculated material from social media accounts of 'old' media outlets and as such was not content generated directly by citizens. So, following this, the capacity for social media to hold police to account might be similarly limited since it might reproduce dominant narratives and does not necessarily create a 'view from below'.

Furthermore, the potential for social media content to provide effective oversight of police action is limited by, among other things, the audience response and reading of images and text. There is a conundrum since the capacity of an individual to elicit public support and sympathy is likely to depend not only on the apparent mistreatment at the hands of the police, but also on the extent to which they are an 'ideal victim'. Established narratives and media processes seem likely to be (at least somewhat) reproduced in social media, just as the media coverage extended to crime victims is influenced to a considerable extent by the degree to which they are a 'perfect' victim in terms of their demographic profile. In the context of hate crime, Mason (2007) has argued that victimisation is constructed in ways that include certain groups but not those considered normatively unacceptable. The capacity of social media to ensure police are held to account is likely also to be limited along such lines. In a rapidly moving, dynamic and highly competitive social media environment, stories that are not 'framed' in ways easily identified and understood by audiences seem unlikely to achieve traction, regardless of the intrinsic nature of the content. Thus, footage of apparent or alleged police violence against political demonstrators, for example, might fit established narratives of popular protest and public order policing and so be easily recognised and understood by social media audiences. More complex, unusual or nuanced police interactions with the public – even if they relate to potentially serious matters of misconduct – might not capture audience attention in the same way.

Bayerl and Stoynov (2016: 1007) explored the power of digital memes to extend transparency over police actions and, by 'framing public discourses about police injustice', to increase the capacity for marginalised groups to hold power to account. Through analysis of a single case study, they highlight that the political and discursive power of social media content is partially determined by technical and aesthetic properties that may not be related to the real-world interactions they represent. In 2011 campus security officers at the University of California pepper-sprayed student protestors who refused to vacate campus premises. An image of one officer spraying a student quickly went viral on social media and was manipulated, photo-shopped and re-presented in other forms relating to other abuses of state power. The considerable replication of the 'pepper-spray cop' meme is explained by Bayerl and Stoynov (2016) in relation to the image's 'content flexibility' (in the sense that the visual image was such that it could be utilised in many contexts) and 'reference flexibility' (since it could be broadened to represent a wide range of abuses of state authority). In these circumstances, social media circulation of the meme contributed to wider political protest against police violence in the US and as such was a relatively effective form of oversight: the officer involved was sacked, although received damages for the stress and psychiatric damage caused by the meme. The traction that the meme achieved arose in part from its recognisability, however. It achieved prominence in the virtual realm since it was easily identifiable and spoke to established narratives of apparent police misconduct. Other images of police misconduct that do not fit established frameworks and representations and are likely to lack 'reference flexibility' so seem unlikely to achieve such prominence.

The capacity for social media to provide meaningful democratic oversight is also limited by the apparent criteria for 'newsworthiness', particularly in relation to the apparent need to have film footage of misconduct. In this way the nature and scope of policing that might be considered problematic become significantly narrowed. Structural or policy-level dimensions of oppressive policing, matters not easily captured on a smart phone, become marginalised since only the operational actions of particular police officers are amenable to the view of the lens. Misconduct, in this context, is construed at the level of the individual officer rather than the police service itself. While this is true of other approaches that respond to allegations of police wrongdoing, for example the complaints and discipline processes reviewed in Chapter 6, there is at least the potential in those processes to address gaps in training, supervision, or management processes in ways not immediately developed by social media footage that reduces officer behaviour to the immediate confines of an incident and removes any wider context. Social media representation of police wrongdoing replicates the 'rotten apples' model of corruption and abuse of power, which focuses attention on the proclivities of deviant officers and ignores the organisational context and culture that can also contribute to misconduct (Chan 1997; Westmarland and Rowe 2018).

For all that this is an important limitation, it might be that the power of individual cases offers 'critical moments' whereby moving images portray realities of police brutality, for example, that would be difficult, if not impossible, to convey in other terms. The iconic images – filmed by a passing motorist – of Rodney King being beaten by LAPD officers by the side of a highway in 1992 had a powerful impact on debates about the policing of African Americans (Gooding-Williams 1993). Nonetheless, three of the officers charged in relation to the case were acquitted on all charges and the jury failed to reach a decision in relation to charges brought against the fourth. Furthermore, the emergence of the Black Lives Matter movement decades later suggests that the King footage did not effect lasting change. It might well be that other mechanisms to hold officers to account also tend not to occasion long-term significant change, and as such this problem is not only related to social media content. Nonetheless it remains a limitation that the power of dramatic footage, captured by citizen journalists, does not always have significant evidential value and does not inevitably lead to better outcomes in terms of social justice. Transparency in and of itself does not equate to justice. Crucially, in the King case, different interpretations of the footage emerged in the public, and legal, debates that followed broadcast, further illustrating that images do not 'speak for themselves' and are inevitably mediated and understood in particular political and social contexts (Crenshaw and Peller 1993).

Conclusion

A fundamental limitation of citizen journalism as a mechanism for addressing police misconduct is that any increased capacity to present matters in the public domain in a relatively short period of time does not necessarily result in a more effective or efficient mechanism to investigate or remedy grievances. Outrage might be generated by clips uploaded to social media but no path to justice necessarily unfolds. As a form of 'soft accountability', the impact of social media is highly dependent on the wider context in which it unfolds. White's (2016) example of G4S being effectively held to account by 'soft' powers of the media, public opinion and politicians in relation to the 2012 Olympic Games provides a good illustration of the potential for informal remedy, but other documented scandals surrounding private sector involvement in criminal justice have not led to reform or restitution. Perhaps the context of the Olympic Games and that soldiers were having leave cancelled so that they could be redeployed to fill the gaps left by G4S provided a narrative such that this case was newsworthy and politically attractive to pursue. 'Soft accountability' might be less effective in other circumstances.

Social media technology has contributed significantly to the scope and capacity of 'citizen journalism'. From police involvement in fatal shootings in the US to more mundane footage of excessive force or apparent misconduct, there have in recent years been numerous examples of members of the public recording and disseminating footage that has held police to account in ways previously unimaginable. Key among these was the case of Ian Tomlinson, who died during protests in London in 2009. In the period between his death and the ensuing trial of PC Harwood (found not guilty of murder), the Metropolitan Police released a previously secret report into the death of Blair Peach, killed during an anti-fascist demonstration in London in 1979. That report acknowledged that Peach had likely been killed by a police officer but could not identify the individual concerned. While drawing comparisons between the two cases is inevitably problematic, the certainty and speed that social media footage of Tomlinson's treatment brought to that case stands in stark contrast to the circumstances in which Peach died. Does this, then, offer a brave new world in which public scrutiny of police offers greater opportunity for accountability? The answer is complex: while many examples seem to suggest an affirmative response, the potential is limited. Not least of the problems is that the independent free spaces of social media are unconnected from any formal mechanisms of accountability. Principles of justice, equity and due process do not apply and so capacity is limited by the extent to which individual cases of wrongdoing can gather attention in the maelstrom of social media. While White (2016) rightly notes that 'critical public discourse' can be a mechanism for accountability, and the earlier discussion notes that there is potential for social media to perform a similar role for policing, it is a route without guarantees in terms of governance and accountability. The wider politics of policing might be shaped by emerging public accounts of misconduct, which can challenge elite discourse in ways that were next to impossible in earlier periods. Nonetheless, they tend overly to focus on particular forms of individual wrongdoing and are at a distance from procedures that might secure justice and reform.

Further reading

Bayerl, P.S. and Stoynov, L. (2016) 'Revenge by Photoshop: Memefying Police Acts in the Public Dialogue about Injustice', *New Media & Society*, 18: 1006–26.

Dymond, A. and Hickman, M. (2017) 'Body-Worn Cameras, Use of Force and Police-Civilian Interactions', *Policing: A Journal of Policy and Practice*, 12: 1–5.

Mann, S. and Ferenbok, J. (2013) 'New Media and the Power Politics of Sousveillance in a Surveillance-Dominated World', *Surveillance and Society*, 11: 18–34.

Sandhu, A. (2017) '"I'm Glad that was on Camera": A Case Study of Police Officers' Perceptions of Cameras', *Policing and Society*, DOI: 10.1080/10439463.2017.1285917.

8

Police accountability and the problem of the public

Changing organisational, legal and political arrangements that hold police services to account have been identified throughout previous chapters. This final chapter considers the political economy of accountability and argues that greater attention needs to be paid to the changing context in which mechanisms developed alongside the modern police in the 19th century currently operate. Key among these are arguments that the position of the nation state – the sovereign source of accountability in traditional models – is weakened in relation to transnational and networked policing (Wood and Shearing 2007). Not only has the relative decline of the nation state meant that governance and accountability have been de-territorialised, it has also meant that private and third-sector agencies have become embedded into practices of policing and regulation such that these become much more difficult to hold to account (Mazerolle and Ransley 2005). As Wood and Shearing (2007) note, power increasingly resides in the relationships between the nodes in a networked policing environment, and not in the nodes themselves. It is more difficult to govern forms of policing that emerge from these relationships, especially since – as previous chapters have demonstrated – mechanisms for accountability have developed around specific policing institutions. The combination of internal and external forms of governance, with low or high degrees of control (as in Romzek and Dubnick's [1987] model of accountability, which has been returned to at many stages in this book), focus on relations between particular agencies and do not extend to the processes of law enforcement and regulation that emerge from policing networks.

The other main focus of the chapter takes the point made by Bowling and Sheptycki (2012), that a challenge for meaningful accountability of transnational policing is that there is not a coherent 'demos' or set of normative standards against which accountability can be applied. The chapter argues, following Reiner (1992, 2015), that this trend is true within the nation state and that neoliberal individualism has brought the 'end of consensus'. This might explain why private or citizen-led mechanisms of accountability (for example civil action against police or social media sousveillance of police practice) seem to have overtaken traditional public responses. These are not just preferred avenues for technical or financial reasons, but they also represent a decline in the possibility of a collective *public* oversight of police work. Consideration of the governance of policing has focused on organisations and mechanisms, and legal and policy matters, and paid insufficient attention to the 'problem' of the public. As is outlined later, a clear mandate or set of normative values relating to the proper outcomes of policing are increasingly difficult to identify in an era of social and political diversity, increasing inequalities, rising individualism and a decline in civic engagement. Prior to considering these debates in greater detail, the chapter outlines some emerging themes in terms of changing structures of police accountability and the increasing pluralisation of policing, both of which trends have implications for the effective governance of policing.

The ethics of policing

These two themes – changing mechanisms of governance and an apparent deterioration in social consensus – reflect a fundamental dichotomy in the philosophy of ethics that distinguishes between consideration of the means by which an outcome is delivered, and examination of the outcomes of a decision. From the former perspective any action is ethical if it is arrived at following a process or a decision that is itself held to be just. This reflects Kant's 'categorical imperative', such that if an action can be understood to be 'good' when applied universally in all circumstances then there is a moral obligation to behave accordingly (Millie 2016). In terms of judging police decisions and actions, the test from this perspective is to consider whether the rules were followed, policies adhered to and the law enacted. Studies of policing that have focused on 'procedural justice' (such that police act in ways consistent with rules and regulations that are themselves understood to be fair and proportionate) have found that this is the most significant determinant of public perceptions of police legitimacy (Hough et al 2013; Bradford 2014; Murphy et al 2014). The latter perspective concentrates on outcomes rather than inputs, and often from a Utilitarian perspective that judges outcomes as just if they produce the greatest happiness for the greatest number. Jeremy Bentham and John Stuart Mill developed the philosophical basis of Utilitarianism on the grounds that the ultimate realisation of human potential was the maximisation of pleasure and the minimisation of pain. Actions that promote this balance are inherently ethical, Utilitarians maintain, although – as is widely noted – a fundamental concern arising from this approach relates to the extent to which suppressing the interests of a small minority can be justified if this maximises the pleasure of the majority (Morrell and Rowe 2019). Philosophically this underpins the concern associated with PCCs and the risk of 'majoritarian authoritarianism' that was discussed in Chapters 2 and 3 drawing on Wood's (2016) distinction between 'democratic' and 'liberal' policing. That there might be formal democracy applied to policing, but that it might remain illiberal, very neatly encapsulates the tension between a 'means' approach to addressing the governance of policing and an 'ends' perspective focused on assessment of the outcomes and impact of policing on the public. The following discussion considers these two approaches to policing the police in further detail, beginning with the challenges identified throughout the book with those measures intended to ensure that the 'means' by which policing is delivered are democratically robust.

Changing structures of accountability

As has been outlined at different stages of the book, many of the established frameworks for police governance in Britain were developed during the middle of the 19th century as modern police services were introduced and expanded nationwide. Both policing and the mechanisms to govern policing emerged during a period when the nation state was expanding and the criminal justice, education and public health arrangements, and local government and civil service organisations and bureaucracies, were being developed. In relation to the police, the organising principle of combined local and national oversight was instigated with Watch Committees and HMIC jointly charged with ensuring forces were effectively resourced. That framework continues as the latter agency continues its role and a succession of other institutions have provided local oversight (including but not limited to police authorities, PCCs, Police and Crime Panels and national agencies in Wales, Scotland and Northern Ireland). It was argued in Chapter 3 that the fact that the role of PCCs has extended horizontally (in that some have expanded to include oversight of fire services, for example) and vertically (in that the APCC is integrated into national police governance arrangements) means that the framework of local and national oversight mechanisms is increasingly unclear. The blurring of this boundary also reflects the growth of cross-service cooperation as the 43 police services of England and Wales co-produce some operational and support services that deliver policing. Policing delivered regionally in these ways is not easily overseen by local PCCs and it seems unlikely that many members of the public would be aware of the technical arrangements for mutual aid or collaborative agreements, and there appears to be no research evidence assessing how joint oversight of such arrangements is discharged in practice. National policing provisions have strengthened across much of the UK in ways that also weaken the powers of local accountability. The creation of Police Scotland as a national force from 2013 removed the local governance arrangements that had applied to the eight services previously operating. While local engagement and consultation continues to be required, it is the responsibility of Police Scotland itself to put this into practice, suggesting they retain considerable power under these arrangements. A similar local democratic deficit applies in England in relation to the National Crime Agency, which is nationally accountable but has considerable powers to coopt local police resources, seemingly without PCCs or PCPs being able to intervene.

While these are some contemporary manifestations of the tensions and contradictions surrounding the local/national model of policing the police, it has been apparent from earlier chapters that they have considerable precedent. Indeed, the principle that the separation of powers prevents any particular institution from becoming over mighty is a foundational touchstone for models of governance in many contexts. Jarvis (2014) argued that avoiding the concentration of power in executive bodies is a core principle of accountability, as was referred to in Chapter 2. However, the increasing pluralisation of policing is arguably a more recent development and, combined with transnational policing, one that poses further challenges to 19th-century models for policing the police.

In many fields of governance and public administration there has been a broad shift from post-Second World War welfare statism, relying on hierarchical delivery (Coates 1995). From telephone services, media, car production, housing, energy and extending into many other dimensions of public and local government services there has been a shift in many western societies, from hierarchical and bureaucratic provisions towards network and market arrangements. Although broader in scope, much of the change has entailed privatisation of public utilities and efforts to promote quasi-market mechanisms into the public sector in an effort to develop greater efficiency through forms of New Public Management reliant on performance indicators that mirror the price mechanism in true market environments (Thompson 1991). These reforms, in Britain at least, impacted on police services later than on health, housing or education (Waddington 1994; McLaughlin and Murji 1997). Nonetheless, wider shifts towards markets and networks have contributed to a neoliberal society in which individuals are made responsible for services and goods once delivered by public organisations. In terms of the policing of the police these developments have posed direct challenges in terms of how private sector security companies and third-party agencies (which are likely to be subject concurrently to competing oversight regimes) should be governed.

It might be that private security has always coexisted with public police and that the attention paid to this sector in recent decades is best thought of as a 're-discovery' rather than a qualitatively new shift (Jones and Newburn 1998). Nonetheless, processes of privatisation in neoliberal societies have afforded significant prominence to private security and created new markets as large corporations and public bodies recruit private companies to regulate access to quasi-public space, to monitor and surveil, and to anticipate and respond to risks and threats. As Lee (2007) indicated, new entrants to the security market have commissioned physical and technological equipment that is routinely deployed in public spaces. Counter-intuitively, perhaps, the 'signal' processes of these public assemblages of security hardware and signage have created new risks and heightened public fear, allowing companies to provide apparent technological solutions to domestic markets. Technological innovation means that the 'locks and bolts' hardware of the late 20th century has been joined by new Wi-Fi-enabled monitoring and alarm systems that apparently 'enable' the homeowner to remain in control of their property from anywhere in the world, for example. That such technology itself poses criminogenic risks is less widely acknowledged, although software companies can provide electronic target-hardening to ameliorate any such concern. As was noted in Chapter 3, the responsibilisation that has been placed on private citizens by government and corporations has also impacted on other sectors of society not traditionally considered as part of law enforcement networks. Financial corporations required to complete Suspicious Activity Reports, universities monitoring student attendance and private landlords vetting prospective tenants are co-joined nodes in law enforcement networks seeking to identify and prevent the financing of terrorism, radicalisation and organised crime.

Along these lines, then, the pluralisation of policing has come to be about much more than the regulation of private security patrols, and as such more complex questions about governance and accountability arise. Considering if policing is delivered in ways consistent with the established rules and regulations – if the means of delivery are properly adhered to – is much more challenging since the actors, and the complex web of arrangements to which they become a party, are diverse and subject to different forms and levels of regulation. Surveillance powers form an important and useful example of these complexities. As we have seen, the public police are subject to the provisions of the Regulation of Investigatory Powers Act, which outlines principles as to when, where and against whom undercover deployment of surveillance technology can be authorised. From a governance point of view a concerned citizen might want (and be able to obtain) reassurance that a particular police service conducted their operations in accordance with these legal requirements. Others involved in policing might not be obliged or so minded. The work of 'Dark Justice' and other vigilante groups seeking to identify and target online paedophiles involves surveillance activities and the publication of undercover recordings of suspected offenders on group websites. Beyond the general remit of the law, none of that activity is regulated or can be held to account as in the case of police operations. This anomaly becomes more significant given that the activities of the vigilante groups increasingly (it seems) combine with the police. Police commentary on this matter often seems ambivalent in the sense that stopping such vigilante activity would be problematic and resource intensive but that it should be discouraged on the grounds of public safety. Nonetheless, it is reported that footage obtained by such groups has been used by prosecutors in around half of cases where the grooming of children for sexual exploitation is alleged (*Guardian* 2018). In a similar vein, police services have developed new protocols and systems to allow road users to provide dash- or head-cam footage of others thought to be committing offences, and frequently appeal for such footage in the aftermath of serious incidents. All of these examples can be subject to debate in terms of public engagement in policing, the impact on police resources and the possibility of individuals being harassed or targeted in some way. All of those are important debates but the significance of these emerging, transient and unstable networks of citizens, social media and tech companies, local authorities and police in terms of governance and accountability is that all are regulated and governed in different ways. Considered in these broad terms, law enforcement and regulation mechanisms that provide internal or external 'hard' accountability in terms of Romzek and Dubnick's (1987) model, focused on discrete elements in these complex networks, are of limited (although important) benefit.

The complexities of these regulatory challenges are made greater by the transnational, even global, status of some of the parties to law enforcement networks. Transnational policing has developed over a long time period and many of the formal arrangements in different regions of the world are subject to governmental oversight in the same way that applies to international law more generally. Cyber-policing, however, provides a good example of the more recent challenges of governance that have been identified at various stages in this book. As the scope, range and pace of cyber-crime have developed in recent years, so, too, the range of actors involved in law enforcement networks has changed. As was noted in Chapter 2, in 2016 the European Police College was formally renamed as the European Union Agency for Law Enforcement Training, with an extended mandate requiring that all sectors (including, for example, border guards, customs and excise departments and fisheries agencies) be included in its remit. A further challenge for those tasked with governance and accountability is to develop the means of incorporating powerful data and social media companies within these frameworks. In Chapter 5 it was noted that recent scandals about data analytics firms interfering in electoral process in various countries demonstrated that the regulatory gap remains a significant challenge as global corporations, with huge financial and legal resources, become further integrated into law enforcement networks.

The preceding paragraphs provide grounds for concern in relation to the notion that just policing is delivered when it is consistent with rules and procedures that themselves are of virtue. If policing is delivered in accordance with the correct 'means' then systems of governance and accountability are properly working. It has been shown that the increasing complexity and instability of pluralised network policing makes that a difficult prospect, especially considering the increasing role of transnational parties. In the following section the other model for considering if effective governance is applied will be examined: that which focuses on the 'ends' of policing, rather than the means by which it is delivered.

The problem of public consent?

Theories of democratic governance have long wrestled with the problem of how to conceptualise 'the people' in whose name authority and sovereignty are lent to the state. As noted in Chapter 2, social contract theorists argued that the legitimacy of the state derives from a tacit agreement that individual citizens surrender a degree of personal freedom to the government in return for the promise of an orderly, peaceful society, with a system of law and other provisions that enable a good life. While such approaches have underpinned liberal democracy through suggesting that political power derives from the people, they have, from the outset, been problematic in terms of how 'the people' is understood. For John Locke, individual rights rooted in property ownership underpin democratic political rights, and women and slaves were excluded from the political class. Indeed, Locke wrote extensively in defence of slave ownership in terms of the broader right of individuals to own property (Farr 2008). Political theorists refer to this as the 'boundary problem': in defining democratic legitimacy in terms of public consent to the authority of the state, how and in what terms is 'the public' understood? Verschoor (2018) noted that traditional approaches that conceived (often only implicitly) of the public in terms of a pre-social population inhabiting a particular territory are increasingly incoherent as the impact of migration is recognised and supra-territorial systems of governance develop. Instead of being a fixed abstraction, the public becomes a dynamic, unstable and contestable category. The re-emergence of forms of nationalism and political nativism in recent years are frequently explained in terms of a 'backlash' against globalisation, which has seen renewed emphasis on prioritising the rights of settled communities of long standing over the claims of more recent migrants. The rejection of migration and the reassertion of nationalism have underpinned – in part – political programmes associated with Brexit, Trump's ambitions to Make America Great Again, and the insularity and xenophobia of Orban's Hungary, Erdoğan's Turkey and Putin's Russia. These might be particular and extreme responses to the boundary problem – seeking to reassert, in their various ways, lost forms of political and cultural identity that provide a comforting narrative of national character to set against changing 'runaway worlds' (Giddens 1999). More widely, and perhaps less obviously, though the boundary problem poses a challenge for governance and accountability not only in relation to which individuals, groups and populations are considered part of the 'demos' in categorical terms, but also more widely in the sense that the normative or ethical basis for consensus may also be increasingly precarious. For these reasons an 'ends' based approach to evaluating policing becomes more challenging without a framework for consensus as to the most appropriate mandate that policing is expected to deliver.

This precarity is rooted in cultural, political, economic and perhaps generational terms as related and mutually reinforcing factors combine to erode the possibility of a public consensus in relation to what might be the desired ends of public policy, including policing. In economic terms, increasing disparities in wealth within national populations are becoming more entrenched and are related to a host of social, health, educational and other inequalities (Wilkinson and Pickett 2009). If police, in Britain at least, seek to recast their mandate around the primacy of protecting vulnerable members of society (as is discussed later), then these inequalities will make a significant difference to the burden of work that the police face and will have an impact on debates about the proper role and priorities for police. Beyond the UK, global inequalities in the distribution of wealth have far-reaching consequences in terms of policing and governance more widely. Poverty, military conflict and environmental degradation combine in many regions and are closely bound up with geopolitics and the economy. Such problems have considerable and immediate consequences in particular regions and countries that experience them – despite the view from Western Europe, the challenges of migration are far more acute in parts of Africa than they are in rich first world economies (Mongae 2017). The externalities of first world economic activities that produce enormous environmental degradation across the Global South pose huge challenges economically, socially and demographically in the countries and regions directly affected but also – crucially – more widely still. As problems of climate change become more entrenched then it is likely that the impact of global warming on Western Europe and in North America will become greater and the economic and social consequences of recent years will accelerate, with consequences for policing as for government more widely. More than a decade ago, the head of the Australian Federal Police stated that climate change, and resultant migration, posed the biggest single threat to law enforcement in Australia (Keelty 2007) and EUROPOL has developed a series of 'third country' partnerships in North Africa in an effort to respond more effectively to migration, terrorism and crime threats emanating from that region.

The neoliberal world order that underpins a framework of free-trade, global competition and restricts the capacity of nation states has not only created a series of interconnected challenges of climate change, security, migration and economic inequality; it has also eroded the possibility of public consensus and engagement which might provide a stronger basis to respond to such existential challenges. This points to a significant conundrum in terms of the developments of accountability in policing that have been charted throughout this book. In broad terms, and notwithstanding continuing challenges, there has been – in Britain and elsewhere – a general trend towards greater transparency and oversight of policing. Some of this has been initiated by police and the state itself and some has arisen through social and technological change. However, and herein lies the rub, the normative basis against which the 'ends' of policing are judged is incoherent and is undermined by political and economic changes occasioned by neoliberalism over recent decades. In his review of the impact of new forms of surveillance on police practice, Brucato (2015: 41) argued that effective accountability requires the combination of several practices:

> Legitimacy, then, requires transparency because rules must be displayed, seen, and understood by publics, and that understanding should result in a perceived coherence between institutional standards and community norms … These rules rely on broadly shared beliefs or norms, and legitimation is formally expressed through public consent, demonstrated through widespread, voluntary submission to the rule of law and its enforcement, and demonstrated by trust in representatives and agents of government.

It is the 'broadly shared beliefs and norms' – the possibility of a 'demos' – that is imperilled by neoliberalism and the gulf of financial, cultural and political inequalities. The privatisation and atomisation of society (Putnam 2001) suggests that the capacity of inchoate, shifting and unstable societies to generate norms or a mandate for policing becomes increasingly restricted. Technological, policy and economic imperatives of recent decades have repositioned citizens such that providing for security (in many forms) becomes a personal responsibility to be achieved through target hardening and behaviour modification. Social or community-based forms of crime prevention, provided collectively through youth services or welfare provisions, have been eschewed as 'designing out crime' and the creation of new forms of aesthetically pleasing public spaces more appropriate to the consumer- and leisure-based economies have been pursued (Coleman 2004; Lee 2007; Millie 2011).

The extension of accountability of policing in England and Wales has included the creation of PCCs and the introduction of new forms of transparency in cases of alleged misconduct. The former represents the extension of a particular, and limited, model of electoral democracy that formally creates all adult citizens as equals. Similarly, public misconduct hearings and the publication online of details of cases and outcomes provides all members of the public with information necessary to make informed choices about police behaviour. As Reiner (2015) argued in relation to PCCs, such reforms focus on extending democracy in electoral terms but do nothing to address the civil or socio-economic rights that are important in themselves, and as preconditions for effective electoral participation. Democratic oversight of policing requires that citizens have knowledge of their rights and how they can be enforced, and access to mechanisms of redress where appropriate. Reiner (2015: 143) characterised the limitations of recent reforms in stark terms, noting that 'elections in a context of vast and accelerating inequality of condition and resources cannot provide real power to the people, in policing or any other policy arena'.

Social, economic and political inequalities undermine the possibility of democratic participation and so lessen the possibility of effective governance of policing. The challenge is not just to create effective legal and institutional arrangements that meet the rapidly evolving circumstances in which policing is delivered, but also to promote – through education, access to information and resources and the promotion of civic engagement – the conditions necessary for diverse publics to engage meaningfully in debate and decision making as to the proper role of policing. Even were this achieved, though, it is likely that the public will, like communities and neighbourhoods at the micro-level, be 'unstable, leaky and unpredictable' (Hughes and Rowe 2007) in terms of articulating normative standards against which policing can be held to account. There are objective differences in terms of experiences of crime and disorder, socio-economic circumstances, geography and demographics that mean different demands and expectations are placed on police by different sections of society. Let alone in broader terms, even at the level of individual police services the breadth and diversity of populations makes it challenging for PCCs in England and Wales to 'represent' local demands for policing, and appeals to the interests of local communities might be a matter of rhetorical legitimisation rather than an objective reflection of public interest. As was noted in Chapter 3, some PCCs are required to 'represent' populations of several million people, spanning dozens of parliamentary constituencies. Diverse populations have different policing needs, demands and standards against which questions of legitimacy, efficiency and governance are examined. Contemporary debates about the use of social media and online platforms as vehicles for the delivery of community policing, which once was organised around local police stations and officers on foot patrol, are often focused on the different demands on police services emanating from particular demographic and geographic cohorts. Those living in rural areas, for example, have been found to have different forms of relations with police than those in urban neighbourhoods (Mawby and Yarwood 2011; Yarwood 2015). The use of social media as an online provider of reassurance policing might be effective with some sections of the community but will have little meaning for those on the wrong side of the digital divide who have no access to cyber space, an exclusion entwined with other forms of social stratification and inequality (Ragnedda 2017).

Even within particular geographic locations, public perceptions of crime and antisocial behaviour more widely can be complex and subjective in ways that mean a singular style or level of policing might meet the expectations of diverse publics. Millie (2011) found that the same forms of behaviour were variously celebrated, tolerated or condemned in urban districts of Toronto, depending on the context in which they occurred and the value judgements, political disposition and aesthetics of individuals. Similarly, Rowe and Hutton (2012) found that public perceptions of graffiti in urban environments are shaped by the ways in which individuals engaged with the city and wider subjective assessments relating to claims of ownership of public space. Much of the work of cultural and critical criminologists in relation to the criminalisation of 'antisocial behaviour' has uncovered the wider political and social inequalities that have underpinned such processes. The intrinsic properties of particular forms of behaviour and the harm to which they give rise provide only a partial explanation for the introduction of policing and criminal justice policy responses. Policing, as conducted by a wide range of agencies and networks, might provide an effective response to social problems but the identification of forms of behaviour considered problematic and amenable to such interventions reflects wider political, social, economic and cultural inequalities. What constitutes an 'effective' response similarly is a highly subjective judgement, and one likely to be answered differently depending on one's wider social experiences.

To a considerable degree, these critical concerns about the limited extent to which there is a widespread normative consensus about the legitimate aims and mandate of policing have applied for many decades. Arguments that police face a crisis of legitimacy need to avoid overstating the degree of consensus that might have existed in earlier periods and the risk of exaggerating the difficulty of developing consensus in contemporary times. Histories of British policing provide considerable evidence of the range and persistence of opposition constabularies faced from their inception onwards (Emsley

1996; Rawlings 2005) and even during the mid twentieth-century 'golden age' of consensus and legitimacy it is clear that problems of corruption, violence and racism were widespread (Whitfield 2004). Notwithstanding that there were problems, sometimes hidden, with British policing from the late 1940s until the 1960s, Reiner (2000) argued that the relatively high levels of public support during that period reflected the wider post-war settlement, the inclusivity of the developing welfare state and a political process that incorporated organised labour. If that social, economic and political settlement provided for consensus, then contemporary neoliberal individualism has undermined the basis of collective identity required for 'public' accountability (Young 1999). Similarly, Putnam (2001) identified ways in which economic and political shifts over the last decades of the 20th century eroded social and cultural bonds and reduced the capacity for collective efficacy and the possibility for normative consensus. The possibility of reaching agreement about what constitutes legitimate, appropriate, or 'good' policing seems, from such perspectives, to become ever reduced. These trends might apply to the provision of any good or service but are particularly challenging for policing, given that public police services embody state sovereignty and play a significant role in the creation and re-creation of citizenship. Practices of stop and search, for example, or border policing, are symbolic and material expressions of the power of the state in defining when and where individuals have a legitimate right of belonging. Bradford (2018: 144) characterised the negative impact that procedural injustice associated with stop and search can have in terms of citizenship status more widely:

> If people perceive that the way police officers treat them is based not on what they are doing but on their race, gender, or age, police behaviour undermines trust and carries negative identity implications, raising critical questions about whether those on the receiving end are accorded rights pertaining to the groups the police represent ... or whether they have been assigned by police to a different group identity that may be less valorized by police, by others in society, and, indeed, by themselves.

Neoliberal individualism, growing inequalities caused by a decline in socio-economic components of democracy and increasing identity politics that accentuates diversity mean that there is an ever-decreasing basis for normative consensus around the proper mandate of policing.

For these reasons, the difficulties of holding police to account – of meaningful governance – increase. However effective new forms of transparency might be, or more rigorous are independent oversight bodies in identifying malpractice, the capacity of contemporary societies to develop a consensus around the proper function and role of police is undermined. In the context of policing, this problem is particularly acute since the policing, at least modern public policing, plays a constitutive role in shaping and reshaping relations between citizens and between the people and state. Understood as the state in uniform, the public police are the operational expression of sovereignty as they exercise power over the public.

The boundary problem of identifying which groups of people are included or excluded as members of the public becomes more complex if understood as an ongoing, partial and unpredictable process: unstable coalitions or communities of interest might emerge around some policing agendas ('cracking down on street crime') but might not transfer to other operational domains ('tackling traffic crime'). Achieving consensus on whether policing has achieved desirable outcomes (even if the required procedures have been observed) becomes more difficult once the changing nature of communities is recognised. As indicated throughout much of this book, liberal democratic approaches to police governance have invoked models of community and public engagement fixed in geographical locations. Just as policing itself has been organised around space – the beat, the command unit, the constabulary – so too have the local and national frameworks of accountability been cast. In late modern societies such place-based models of community become increasingly anachronistic. Technology and globalisation, cultural and political change, have combined to replace what Young (1999) referred to as 'ideal communities' with 'low intensity communities'. The former tend to be defined in spatial terms, to be relatively fixed and homogeneous, and offer a relatively predictable normative consensus around which policing might be organised. The latter are characterised by fluidity, are organised around culture and identity (rather than place), and are more mobile. As a basis for democratic governance, low-intensity communities offer a much less predictable and less fixed agenda.

While it seems likely that structural changes in contemporary societies make political and social consensus more difficult, it must be recognised that the nature and quality of consensus during earlier periods – the golden age – of policing were problematic in many respects. Not only (as was noted earlier) is there considerable evidence of contemporaneous concerns about police malpractice, it is apparent that for many sections of society the police (and the criminal justice system and state institutions more widely) not only offered little protection from criminal harm, but were often agents of harassment and discrimination. The racist victimisation of Black, Asian and Minority Ethnic communities was not only overlooked by police services for many decades; police officers participated in harassment through the abuse of 'sus' powers in ways that criminalised large sections of those communities (Solomos 1988; Keith 1993). Victims of domestic abuse and sexual assault were similarly failed (Edwards 1989) – to a considerable extent – by police services and other agencies for many decades, and homosexuals were widely targeted by police (Burke 1993; Moran 2012). From the perspective of large swathes of society, it seems unlikely that earlier decades represented a consensual period for police–public relations. In these terms the increased recognition of identity politics might better be understood as the articulation of rights claims rather than an erosion of wider consensus. The demand is that previously marginalised communities of interest are afforded the same level of recognition that the state, the criminal justice system and the police have in principle – but not in practice – offered universally to all citizens (Young 1999).

This recognition further reminds that increasing recognition of diversity and pluralism, and that communities are more 'lightly engaged' than in earlier periods, does not mean the wholesale dissolution of social consensus. Normative demands around the mandate of policing are more difficult, less predictable and more fluid, but not entirely absent. Identifying an ethically just policing system in terms of the outcomes delivered, rather than the means of delivery, might be more difficult in a diverse and fragmented society but common normative values are not wholly lost. Although Putnam (2001) identified the decline of forms of social and cultural capital that led to a decline in community engagement associated with mid twentieth-century US society, other dynamics and mechanisms have emerged such that the nature of communities has changed but not been eroded. Nonetheless, as has been noted repeatedly throughout this book, concerns about the governance of policing are closely bound up with wider concerns about public dissatisfaction with political processes, corrupt business practices, untrustworthy media and institutional malpractice in charitable and religious contexts. The 'crisis of trust' in western democratic societies has been identified for a considerable period (van der Meer [2017] traces contemporary concerns back to the 1970s) and has taken different forms across a range of circumstances during this time (Seyd 2015). Declining levels of public trust in broad terms undermine specific efforts at police reform in developing societies (Goldsmith 2005) since trust is regarded as a necessary precondition for legitimacy and public granting of authority to police services. If trust is declining in developed liberal democracies then similar implications seem likely to follow for police services. Although British police services have tended to command relatively high levels of public confidence (relative to other institutions or professions, for example) declining levels of trust in wider terms, coupled with a wider decline in deference and the erosion of traditional communities, seem likely to make the challenge of identifying the proper mandate of policing ever more problematic.

Necessary but unstable: public accountability and police futures

The governance of policing in Britain and elsewhere has been transformed in recent years in terms of the overt organisational, legal and constitutional apparatus developed for such purposes but also because of technological, social and cultural transformation. As noted at the very outset of this book, the central challenge in policing the police has traditionally revolved around the combination of police discretion and the capacity of officers to engage in deviant behaviour of various kinds. Both components of the problem persist. Discretion is an inevitable and desirable feature of the police officer role in a free society. Forms of police deviance might take new forms (as has happened in relation to data integrity) but the role of police places officers in public, private and third-party organisations in circumstances where such opportunities are likely to be available. However, it has been shown that in various ways the extent to which public policing is carried out in conditions of low visibility has been reduced through more proactive management systems and emerging forms of sousveillance. Transparency – and the principle that sunlight is the best disinfectant – has enhanced the visibility of police behaviour, and accountability is increased through technical systems that monitor and record officer activity.

It has also been demonstrated that the new forms of accountability – internal as well as external, 'hard' as well as 'soft' – continue to be hedged with uncertainties and limitations. It is clear that public oversight does not effectively extend to private and third-party policing activities, and transnational policing is inherently beyond the scope of state-centred governance. Big data, predictive and evidence-based policing strategies all pose challenges since the technocratic approach to enhancing policing might be in tension with traditions of community oversight. Democratic control of such strategies will remain a contentious challenge of the future, just as other professionalisation agendas have been in the past. It has been argued earlier that a further set of problems relates to the increasing pluralisation and consciousness of diversity in terms of low-intensity communities that fail to provide a solid consensus around the proper mandate of policing. Not only are accountability mechanisms becoming more complex; so, too, is the public on whose behalf the police are policed. In such circumstances, the solution cannot be to abandon as too difficult efforts to govern policing in the public interest or to preserve a sense of policing as a public good. To do so would relinquish any capacity of policing to respond to criminal, social and environmental harms that will threaten vulnerable communities and populations domestically and globally. Consultation, governance and accountability of policing needs to continue to address public interest and demand, even though it is recognised that such sources of legitimacy are likely to offer conditional, temporary and partial mandates for policing.

Further reading

Bowling, B. and Sheptycki, J. (2012) *Global Policing*, London: Sage.

Reiner, R. (1992) 'Policing a Postmodern Society', *Modern Law Review*, 55: 761–78.

Wilkinson, R.G. and Pickett, K. (2009) *The Spirit Level: Why More Equal Societies Almost Always Do Better*, London: Allen Lane.

References

Antony, M.G. and Thomas, R.J. (2010) '"This is Citizen Journalism at its Finest": YouTube and the Public Sphere in the Oscar Grant Shooting Incident', *New Media & Society*, 12: 1280–96.

Argyrous, G. (2012) 'Evidence Based Policy: Principles of Transparency and Accountability', *Australian Journal of Public Administration*, 71: 457–68.

Ariel, B., Sutherland, A., Henstock, D., Young, J., Drover, P., Sykes, J., Megicks, S. and Henderson, R. (2017) '"Contagious Accountability": A Global Multisite Randomized Controlled Trial on the Effect of Police Body-Worn Cameras on Citizens' Complaints Against the Police', *Criminal Justice and Behaviour*, 44: 293–316.

Babuta, A. (2017) *Big Data and Policing: An Assessment of Law Enforcement Requirements, Expectations and Priorities*, London: Royal United Services Institute.

Bailey, V. (ed) (1981) *Policing and Punishment in Nineteenth Century Britain*, London: Croom Helm.

Baldry, A.C. and Sebire, J. (2016) 'Policing and Domestic Abuse: Challenges and Ways to Go', *Policing: A Journal of Policy and Practice*, 10: 323–27.

Banton, M. (1964) *The Policeman in the Community*, London: Tavistock Publications.

Bauman, Z. (2000) 'Social Issues of Law and Order', *British Journal of Criminology*, 40: 205–21.

Bayerl, P.S. and Stoynov, L. (2016) 'Revenge by Photoshop: Memefying Police Acts in the Public Dialogue about Injustice', *New Media & Society*, 18: 1006–26.

BBC (2015) 'Leicestershire Police "Ignore" Attempted Burglaries at Odd-Numbered Houses', http://www.bbc.co.uk/news/uk-england-leicestershire-33788264, accessed 19 April 2018.

BBC (2018) '2,000 Wrongly Matched with Possible Criminals at Champions League', https://www.bbc.co.uk/news/uk-wales-south-west-wales-44007872, accessed 8 February 2019.

Becker, H.S. (1963) *Outsiders: Studies in the Sociology of Deviance*, New York: The Free Press.

Becker, H.S. (1967) 'Whose Side Are We On?', *Social Problems*, 14: 239–47.

Bovens, M. (2007) 'Analysing and Assessing Accountability: A Conceptual Framework', *European Law Journal*, 13: 447–68.

Bowling, B. and Sheptycki, J. (2012) *Global Policing*, London: Sage.

Bowling, B. and Sheptycki, J. (2016) 'reflections on Legal and Political Accountability for Global Policing', in Lister, S. and Rowe, M. (eds) *Accountability of Policing*, pp. 214–30.

Brain, T. (2000) *A History of Policing in England and Wales from 1974*, Oxford: Oxford University Press.

Bradford, B. (2014) 'Policing and Social Identity: Procedural Justice, Inclusion and Cooperation between Police and Public', *Policing and Society*, 24: 22–43.

Bradford, B. (2018) *Stop and Search and Police Legitimacy*, London: Routledge.

Brodeur, J-P. (1983) 'High Policing and Low Policing: Remarks about the Policing of Political Activities', *Social Problems*, 30: 507–20.

Brodeur, J-P. (2007) 'High and Low Policing in Post-9/11 Times', *Policing*, 1: 25–37.

Brucato, B. (2015) 'The New Transparency: Police Violence in the Context of Ubiquitous Surveillance', *Media and Communication*, 3: 39–55.

Bruns, A., Highfield, T. and Burgess, J. (2013) 'The Arab Spring and Social Media Audiences: English and Arabic Twitter Users and Their Networks', *American Behavioral Scientist*, 57(7): 871–98.

Bunyan, T. (1977) *The Political Police in Britain*, London: Quartet Books.

Burke, M.E. (1993) *Coming Out of the Blue*, London: Continuum.

Burney, E. (2009) *Making People Behave: Anti-Social Behaviour, Politics and Policy*, second edition, Cullompton: Willan.

Burrell, J. (2016) 'How the Machine Thinks: Understanding Opacity in Machine Learning Algorithms', *Big Data & Society*, 3: 1–12.

Cain, M. (1973) *Society and the Policeman's Role*, London: Routledge and Kegan Paul.

Caless. B. and Owens, J. (2016) *Police and Crime Commissioners: The Transformation of Police Accountability*, Bristol: Policy Press.

Carrabine, E. (2012) 'Just Images: Aesthetics, Ethics and Visual Criminology', *British Journal of Criminology*, 52(3): 463–89.

Chambers S. (2014) 'Who is Policing the Police and Crime Commissioners?', *Safer Communities*, 13: 32–9.

Chan, H.S. and Rosenbloom, D.H. (2010) 'Four Challenges to Accountability in Contemporary Public Administration: Lessons from the United States and China', *Administration and Society*, 42(1): 11S–33S.

Chan, J. (1997) *Changing Police Culture: Policing in a Multicultural Society*, Melbourne: Cambridge University Press.

Chan, J. (1999) 'Governing Police Practice: Limits of the New Accountability', *British Journal of Sociology*, 50: 251–70.

Chan, J. (2003) *Fair Cop: Learning the Art of Policing*, Toronto: Toronto University Press.

Chapman, C. (2014) *An Independent Review of the Police Disciplinary System in England and Wales*, London: Home Office.

Chen, T., Wu, F., Luo, T.T., Wang, M. and Ho, Q. (2016) 'Big Data Management and Analytics for Mobile Crowd Sensing', *Mobile Information Systems*, doi:10.1155/2016/8731802.

Chibnall, S. (1977) *Law-and-Order News: An Analysis of Crime Reporting in the British Press*, London: Tavistock Press.

Coates, D. (1995) *Running the Country*, London: Sage Publications.

Cockbain, E. (2013) 'Grooming and the "Asian Sex Gang Predator": the Construction of a Racial Crime Threat', *Race and Class*, 54: 22–32.

Coleman, R. (2004) *Reclaiming the Streets: Surveillance, Social Control and the City*, Cullompton: Willan.

Coleman, R. (2005) 'Surveillance in the City: Primary Definition and Urban Spatial Order', *Crime, Media, Culture*, 1: 131–48.

Conaghan, J. (2017) 'Investigating Rape: Human Rights and Police Accountability', *Legal Studies*, 37: 54–77.

Crawford, A. (2003) 'The Pattern of Policing in the UK: Policing Beyond the Police', in Newburn, T. (ed) *Handbook of Policing*, Cullompton: Willan Publishing, pp. 136–68.

Crawford, A. (2017) 'Research Co-Production and Knowledge Mobilisation in Policing' in Knutsson, J. and Tompson, L. (eds) *Advances in Evidence-Based Policing*, Abingdon: Routledge, pp. 195–213.

Crawford, A. and Lister S. (2006) 'Additional Security Patrols in Residential Areas: Notes from the Marketplace', *Policing and Society*, 16: 164–88.

Crawford, K. and Calo, R. (2016) 'There is a Blind Spot in AI Research', *Nature*, 538: 311–13.

Crenshaw, K. and Peller, G. (1993) 'Reel Time/Real Justice', *Denver University Law Review*, 70: 283–96.

Critchley, T.A. (1978) *A History of Police in England and Wales*, second edition, London: Constable.

Dein, J. (2000) 'Police Misconduct Revisited', *Criminal Law Review*, October: 801–13.

Disney, R. and Simpson, P. (2017) *Police Workforce and Funding in England and Wales*, London: Institute for Fiscal Studies.

Dubnick, M.J. (2002) 'Seeking Salvation for Accountability', paper presented at the Annual Meeting of the American Political Science Association.

Dymond, A. and Hickman, M. (2017) 'Body-Worn Cameras, Use of Force and Police-Civilian Interactions', *Policing: A Journal of Policy and Practice*, 12: 1–5.

Eaton, D. (2015) 'Making the Shift: Leading First with Who We Are, Not What We Do', *People and Strategy*, 38(3): 46–9.

Edwards, A. (2016) 'Multi-centred Governance and Circuits of Power in Liberal Modes of Security', *Global Crime*, 17(3/4): 240–63.

Edwards, S. (1989) *Policing 'Domestic' Violence: Women, the Law, and the State*, London: Sage.

Edwards, S. (2009) 'Commons and Crowds: Figuring Photography from Above and Below', *Third Text*, 23(4): 447–64.

Ellison, G. (2007) 'A Blueprint for Democratic Policing Anywhere in the World? Police Reform, Political Transition, and Conflict Resolution in Northern Ireland', *Police Quarterly*, 10(3): 243–69.

Emsley, C. (1996) *The English Police: Political and Social History*, second edition, London: Longman.

Ericson, R. and Haggerty, K. (1997) *Policing the Risk Society*, Oxford: Clarendon Press.

Evans, R. and Lewis, P. (2013) *Undercover: the True Story of Britain's Secret Police*, London: Faber and Faber.

Farr, J. (2008) 'Locke, Natural Law, and New World Slavery', *Political Theory*, 36: 495–522.

Ferguson, A.G. (2017) *The Rise of Big Data Policing: Surveillance, Race and the Future of Law Enforcement*, New York: New York University Press.

Ferrell, J., Hayward, K. and Young, J. (2008) *Cultural Criminology: An Invitation*, London: Sage.

Fichtelberg, A. (2015) 'Democratic Policing and State Capacity in an Integrated World' in Andreopoulos, G. (ed) *Policing Across Borders: Law Enforcement Networks and the Challenges of Crime Control*, New York: Springer Verlag, pp. 11–26.

Flanagan, A. (2016) *Review of Police Governance*, Glasgow: Scottish Police Authority.

Fleming, J. and Rhodes, R.A.W. (2005) 'Bureaucracy, Contracts and Networks: The Unholy Trinity and the Police', *The Australian and New Zealand Journal of Criminology*, 38: 192–205.

Fleming, J. and Wingrove, J. (2017) '"We Would If We Could ... but Not Sure If We Can": Implementing Evidence-Based Practice: The Evidence-Based Practice Agenda in the UK', *Policing: A Journal of Policy and Practice*, 11: 202–13.

Gadd, D. and Jefferson, T. (2009) 'Anxiety, Defensiveness and the Fear of Crime' in Lee, M. and Farrall, S. (eds) *Fear of Crime: Critical Voices in an Age of Anxiety*, New York: Routledge, pp. 125–42.

Garland, D. (2001) *The Culture of Control*, Oxford: Oxford University Press.

Garvie, C. and Frankle, J. (2016) 'Facial Recognition Software Might Have a Racial Bias Problem', *The Atlantic*, 7 April.

Giddens, A. (1999) *Runaway World: How Globalisation Is Reshaping Our Lives*, London: Profile.

Goldsmith, A. (2005) 'Police Reform and the Problem of Trust', *Theoretical Criminology*, 9: 443–70.

Goldsmith, A. (2010) 'Policing's New Visibility', *British Journal of Criminology*, 50: 914–34.

Goldstein, H. (1964) 'Police Discretion: the Ideal Versus the Real', *Public Administration Review*, 23, 140–8.

Goldstein, J. (1960) 'Police Discretion Not to Invoke the Criminal Process: Low-Visibility Decisions in the Administration of Justice', *Yale Law Journal*, 69, 543–94.

Goode, J. and Lumsden, K. (2018) 'The McDonaldisation of Police-Academic Partnerships: Organisational and Cultural Barriers Encountered in Moving from Research *on* Police to Research *with* Police', *Policing & Society: an International Journal of Research & Policy*, 28: 75–89.

Gooding-Williams, R. (1993) *Reading Rodney King, Reading Urban Uprising*, New York: Routledge.

Guardian (2018) 'Evidence From "Paedophile Hunters" Used to Charge Suspects 150 Times in Last Year', 10 April, https://www.theguardian.com/uk-news/2018/apr/10/paedophile-hunters-vigilantes-police-evidence-grooming, accessed 11 December 2018.

Grant, S. and Rowe, M. (2011) 'Running the Risk: Police Officer Discretion and Family Violence in New Zealand', *Policing and Society*, 21: 1–18.

Greater Manchester Police Authority (2011) *Report of the Chief Constable to the Quality of Service Committee 24 June 2011*, https://meetings.gmpcc.org.uk/documents/s752/Legal%20Services%20update%20final.pdf, accessed 5 April 2018.

Greer, C. and McLaughlin, E. (2010) 'We Predict a Riot?: Public Order Policing, New Media Environments and the Rise of the Citizen Journalist', *The British Journal of Criminology*, 50: 1041–59.

Gunter, A. (2016) *Race, Gangs and Youth Violence: Policy, Prevention and Policing*, Bristol: Policy Press.

Hadjimatheou, K. (2017) 'Neither Confirm nor Deny: Secrecy and Disclosure in Undercover Policing', *Criminal Justice Ethics*, 36: 279–96.

Hales, G. (2015) 'A Question of Confidence: Reflections on the Case of Nick Gargan', The Police Foundation, http://www.police-foundation.org.uk/2015/10/a-question-of-confidence-reflections-on-the-case-of-nick-gargan/, accessed 9 March 2018.

Harcourt, B. (2007) *Against Prediction – Profiling, Policing and Punishing in an Actuarial Age*, Chicago: University of Chicago Press.

Harper, D. (1988) 'Visual Sociology: Expanding Sociological Vision', *The American Sociologist*, 19(1): 54–70.

Hearnden, I. and May, T. (2013) *Local Resolution of Police Complaints: The Views of Complainants. A Report to the Independent Police Complaints Commission*, London: IPCC.

Her Majesty's Inspectorate of Constabulary (2014) *Police Integrity and Corruption Inspection Data*, London: HMICFRS, https://www.justiceinspectorates.gov.uk/hmicfrs/data/police-integrity-and-corruption-inspection-data/, accessed 29 March 2018.

Holdaway, S. (2017) 'The Re-Professionalization of the Police in England and Wales', *Criminology & Criminal Justice*, 17: 588–604.

Home Affairs Committee (2013a) *Police and Crime Commissioners: Power to Remove Chief Constables*, London: House of Commons.

Home Affairs Committee (2013b) *Independent Police Complaints Commission*, London: House of Commons.

Home Affairs Committee (2013c) *Independent Police Complaints Commission: IPCC Response to the Committee's Eleventh Report of Session 2012–13*, London: House of Commons.

Home Affairs Committee (2013d) *Independent Police Complaints Commission: Eleventh Report of Session 2012–13, Volume II Additional Written Evidence*, London: House of Commons.

Home Office (2010) *Policing in the 21st Century: Reconnecting Police and the People*, London: Home Office.

Home Office (2017) *Police Workforce, England and Wales, 30 September 2016*, Statistical Bulletin 02/17, London: Home Office.

Hope, T. (2009) 'The Illusion of Control: A Response to Professor Sherman', *Criminology and Criminal Justice*, 9: 125–34.

Hough, M., Jackson, J. and Bradford, B. (2013) 'The Drivers of Police Legitimacy: Some European Research', *Journal of Policing, Intelligence and Counter Terrorism*, 8: 144–65.

Hough, M., May, T., Hales, G. and Belur, J. (2018) 'Misconduct by Police Leaders in England and Wales: an Exploratory Study', *Policing and Society*, 28: 541–52.

Howard, P.N. and Hussain, M.M. (2013) *Democracy's Fourth Wave?: Digital Media and the Arab Spring*, Oxford: Oxford University Press.

Huberts, L.W.J.C., Kaptein, M. and Lasthuizen, K. (2007) 'A Study of the Impact of Three Leadership Styles on Integrity Violations Committed by Police Officers', *Policing: An International Journal of Police Strategies & Management*, 30: 587–607.

Hughes, G. and Rowe, M. (2007) 'Neighbourhood Policing and Community Safety: Researching the Instabilities of the Local Governance of Crime, Disorder and Security in Contemporary UK', *Criminology and Criminal Justice*, 7: 317–46.

Independent Commission on Policing for Northern Ireland (1999) *A New Beginning: Policing in Northern Ireland*, Belfast: Northern Ireland Office.

Independent Police Complaints Commission (2015) *Referring Complaints, Conduct Matters and Death or Serious Injury Matters to the IPCC – a Review of Current Police Force Practice*, London: IPCC.

Independent Police Complaints Commission (2017) *Police Complaints: Statistics for England and Wales 2016/17*, London: IPCC.

Independent Police Complaints Commission (2018) *Annual Report and Statement of Accounts 2016/17*, London: IPCC.

Innes, M. (2013) *Rebooting the PC: Using Innovation to Drive Smart Policing*, London: Policy Exchange.

Ipsos MORI (2016) *Public Confidence in the Police Complaints System*, London: Ipsos MORI.

IRR (Institute of Race Relations) (1979) *Policing Against Black People*, London: IRR.

Jackson, R. (2009) *Review of Civil Litigation Costs: Final Report*, London: Ministry of Justice.

James, A. (2016) *Understanding Police Intelligence Work*, Bristol: Policy Press.

Jarvis, M.D. (2014) 'The Black Box of Bureaucracy: Interrogating Accountability in the Public Service', *Australian Journal of Public Administration*, 73(4): 450–66.

Jefferson, T. and Grimshaw, R. (1984) *Controlling the Constable: Police Accountability in England and Wales*, London: Frederick Muller.

Jessop, B. (2016) 'State Theory' in Ansell, C.K. and Torfing, J. (eds) *Handbook on Theories of Governance*, Cheltenham: Edward Elgar Publishing, pp. 70–85.

Joh, E.E. (2014) 'Policing by Numbers: Big Data and the Fourth Amendment', *Washington Law Review*, 89: 35–68.

Johnston, L. (1992) *The Re-Birth of Private Policing*, London: Routledge.

Johnston, L. and Shearing, C. (2003) *Governing Security: Explorations in Policing and Justice*, London: Routledge.

Jones, J. (2018) *Gosport War Memorial Hospital: The Report of the Gosport Independent Panel*, London: House of Commons.

Jones, T. and Newburn, T. (1998) *Private Security and Public Policing*, Oxford: Clarendon Press.

Jos, P.H. (2006) 'Social Contract Theory: Implications for Professional Ethics', *The American Review of Public Administration*, 36: 139–55.

Judge, A. (1986) 'The Provisions in Practice', in Benyon, J. and Bourn, C. (eds) *Police: Powers, Proprieties and Procedures*, Oxford: Pergamon Press, pp. 175–82.

Kääriäinen, J., Lintonen, T., Laitinen, A. and Pollock, J. (2008) 'The "Code of Silence": Are Self-Report Surveys a Viable Means for Studying Police Misconducts?', *Journal of Scandinavian Studies in Criminology and Crime Prevention*, 9: 86–96.

Kaptein, M. (2008) 'Developing and Testing a Measure for the Ethical Culture of Organizations: the Corporate Ethical Virtues Model', *Journal of Organizational Behaviour*, 29: 923–47.

Kaptein, M. (2011) 'Understanding Unethical Behaviour by Unravelling Ethical Culture', *Human Relations*, 64: 843–69.

Keats Citron, D. and Pasquale, F. (2014) 'The Scored Society: Due Process for Automated Predictions', *Washington Law Review*, 89: 1–33.

Keelty, M. (2007) *Facing the Future: Challenges for Australian Policing in a Globalised World, Ray Whitrod Memorial Oration*, Adelaide: Australia and New Zealand Society of Criminology Annual Conference, 24 September.

Keith, M. (1988) 'Squaring Circles? Consultation and "Inner City" Policing', *New Community*, 15(1): 63–77.

Keith, M. (1993) *Race, Riots and Policing – Lore and Disorder in a Multiracist Society*, London: UCL Press.

Kempa, M., Stenning, P. and Wood, J. (2004) 'Policing Communal Spaces: A Reconfiguration of the "Mass Private Property" Hypothesis', *British Journal of Criminology*, 44: 562–81.

Kitchin, R. (2014) *The Data Revolution: Big Data, Open Data, Data Infrastructures and Their Consequences*, London: Sage.

Klockars, C.B. (1985) 'The Dirty Harry Problem' in Elliston, F.A. and Feldberg, M. (eds) *Moral Issues in Police Work*, Totowa, New Jersey: Rowan and Allanheld.

Kroll, J.A., Huey, J., Barocas, S., Felten, E.W., Reidenberg, J.R, Robinson, D.G and Yu, H. (2017) 'Accountable Algorithms', *University of Pennsylvania Law Review*, 165: 633–705.

Law Society (2017) *Access Denied? LASPO Four Years On: a Law Society Review*, London: Law Society.

Lee, M. (2007) *Inventing Fear of Crime: Criminology and the Politics of Anxiety*, Cullompton: Willan.

Lee, M. and Farrall, S. (eds) (2009) *Fear of Crime: Critical Voices in an Age of Anxiety*, New York: Routledge.

Lepri, B., Oliver, N., Letouzé, E., Pentland, A. and Vinck, P. (2018) 'Fair, Transparent, and Accountable Algorithmic Decision-making Processes: The Premise, the Proposed Solutions, and the Open Challenges', *Philosophy and Technology*, 31: 611–27.

Lewis, P. and Evans, R. (2013) *Undercover: The True Story of Britain's Secret Police*, London: Guardian Books.

Liang, F., Das, V., Kostyuk, N. and Hussain, M.M. (2018) 'Constructing a Data-Driven Society: China's Social Credit System and a State Surveillance Infrastructure', *Policy and Internet*, 10: 415–53.

Lipsky, M. (1980) *Street-level Bureaucracy: Dilemmas of the Individual in Public Services*, New York: Russell Sage Foundation.

Lister, S. (2013) 'The New Politics of the Police: Police and Crime Commissioners and the "Operational Independence" of the Police', *Policing*, 7: 239–47.

Lister, S. (2014) 'Scrutinising the role of the Police and Crime Panel in the New Era of Police Governance in England and Wales', *Safer Communities*, 14: 22–31.

Lister, S. and Jones, T. (2016) 'Plural Policing and the Challenge of Democratic Accountability' in Lister, S. and Rowe, M. (eds) *Accountability of Policing*, London: Routledge, pp. 192–213.

Lister, S. and Rowe, M. (2015) 'Electing Police and Crime Commissioners in England and Wales: Prospecting for the Democratisation of Policing', *Policing and Society*, 25: 358–77.

Lister, S. and Rowe, M. (eds) (2016) *Accountability of Policing*, London: Routledge.

Loader, I. (2014) 'Why Do the Police Matter? Beyond the Myth of Crime Fighting' in Brown, J. (ed) *The Future of Policing*, Abingdon: Routledge, pp. 40–51.

Loader, I. and Mulcahy, A. (2001a) 'The Power of Legitimate Naming: Part I – Chief Constables as Social Commentators in Post-War England', *British Journal of Criminology*, 41: 41–55.

Loader, I. and Mulcahy, A. (2001b) 'The Power of Legitimate Naming: Part II Making Sense of the Elite Police Voice', *British Journal of Criminology*, 41: 22–65.

Loader, I. and Walker, N. (2007) *Civilising Security*, Cambridge: Cambridge University Press.

Loveday, B. (2005) 'The Challenge of Police Reform in England and Wales', *Public Money and Management*, 25: 275–81.

Loveday, B. (2013) 'Police and Crime Commissioners: the Changing Landscape of Police Governance in England and Wales: their Potential Impact on Local Accountability, Police Service Delivery and Community Safety', *International Journal of Police Science and Management*, 15: 22–9.

Lubbers, E. (2015) 'Undercover Research: Corporate and Police Spying on Activists: an Introduction to Activist Intelligence as a New Field of Study', *Surveillance & Society*, 13: 338–53.

Lumsden, K. and Black, A. (2018) 'Austerity Policing, Emotional Labour and the Boundaries of Police Work', *British Journal of Criminology*, 58: 606–23.

Lustgarten, L. (1986) *The Governance of Police*, London: Sweet and Maxwell.

Mann, S. and Ferenbok, J. (2013) 'New Media and the Power Politics of Sousveillance in a Surveillance-Dominated World', *Surveillance and Society*, 11: 18–34.

Manning, P.K. (1982) 'Producing Drama: Symbolic Communication and the Police', *Symbolic Interaction*, 5: 223–42.

Marshall, G. (1965) *Police and Government*, London: Methuen.

Marshall, T.H. (1950) *Citizenship and Social Class*, Cambridge: Cambridge University Press.

Marshall, D. and Thomas, T. (2017) *Privacy and Criminal Justice*, London: Palgrave Macmillan.

Marx, G.T. (2009) 'A Tack in the Shoe and Taking Off the Shoe: Neutralization and Counter-Neutralization Dynamics, *Surveillance and Society*, 6(3): 294–306.

Mason, G. (2007) 'Hate Crime as Moral Category: Lessons from the Snowtown Case', *Australian and New Zealand Journal of Criminology*, 40: 249–71.

Mawby, R.C. (2009) 'Understanding Criminal Justice Through Analysing its Communication', *Criminal Justice Matters*, 78: 15–17.

Mawby, R.I. and Yarwood, R. (eds) (2011) *Rural Policing and Policing the Rural: a Constable Countryside?*, Farnham: Ashgate.

Mazerolle, L. and Ransley, J. (2005) *Third Party Policing*, Cambridge: Cambridge University Press.

McCulloch, J. and Palmer, D. (2007) *Civil Litigation by Citizens against Australian Police between 1994 and 2002*, Canberra: Criminology Research Council.

McLaughlin, E. (1991) 'Police Accountability and Black People: into the 1990s' in Cashmore, E. and McLaughlin, E. (eds) *Out of Order? Policing Black People*, London: Routledge, pp: 109–33.

McLaughlin, E. (2007) *The New Policing*, London: Sage.

McLaughlin, E., Muncie, J. and Hughes, G. (2001) 'The Permanent Revolution: New Labour, New Public Management and the Modernization of Criminal Justice', *Criminal Justice*, 1(3) pp. 301–18.

McLaughlin, E. and Murji, K. (1997) 'The Future Lasts a Long Time: Public Policework and the Managerialist Paradox' in Francis, P., Davies, P. and Jupp, V. (eds) *Policing Futures*, Basingstoke: Macmillan, pp. 80–103.

Metropolitan Police Service (2017) *Malfeasance Claims Against the MPS for the Past Five Years*, https://www.met.police.uk/globalassets/foi-media/disclosure_2017/may_2017/information-rights-unit--malfeasance-claims-against-the-mps-for-the-past-five-years, accessed 5 April 2018.

Miller, J. (2003) *Police Corruption in England and Wales: An Assessment of Current Evidence*, Home Office Online Report 11/03. London: Home Office.

Millie, A. (2008) 'Anti-Social Behaviour, Behavioural Expectations and an Urban Aesthetic', *British Journal of Criminology*, 48: 379–94.

Millie, A. (2011) 'Value Judgments and Criminalization', *The British Journal of Criminology*, 51: 278–95.

Millie, A. (2013) 'The Policing Task and the Expansion (and Contraction) of British Policing', *Criminology and Criminal Justice*, 13: 143–60.

Millie, A. (2016) *Philosophical Criminology*, Bristol: Policy Press.

Mongae, M. (2017) *Violent Conflict and International Migration in Africa, 2005–2013: Empirical Patterns and Government Challenges*, Johannesburg: University of the Witwatersrand.

Moran, L. (2012) 'The Changing Landscape of Policing Male Sexualities; a Minor Revolution?' in Johnson, P. and Dalton, D. (eds) *Policing Sex*, London: Routledge, pp. 11–22.

Morrell, K. and Rowe, M. (2020) 'Democracy, Accountability and Evidence-Based Policing: Who Calls the Shots?' in Fielding, N., Holdaway, S. and Bullock, K. (eds) *Critical Reflections on Evidence-Based Policing*, London: Routledge.

Murphy, K., Mazerolle, L. and Bennett, S. (2014) 'Promoting Trust in Police: Findings from a Randomised Experimental Field Trial of Procedural Justice Policing', *Policing and Society*, 24: 405–24.

Nash, M. (1999) 'Enter the "Polibation Officer"', *International Journal of Police Science and Management*, 1: 360–8.

Newburn, T. (1999) *Understanding and Preventing Police Corruption: Lessons from the Literature*, London: Home Office.

Newburn, T. and Hayman, S. (2002) *Policing, Surveillance and Social Control: CCTV and Police Monitoring of Suspects*, Cullompton: Willan Publishing.

Neyroud, P.W. (2011) *Review of Police Leadership and Training*, London: Home Office.

Neyroud, P. and Beckley, A. (2001) *Policing, Ethics and Human Rights*, Cullompton: Willan Publishing.

Osborne, D. and Gaebler, T. (1992) *Reinventing Government: How the Entrepreneurial Spirit is Transforming the Public Sector*, New York: NY Plume.

Pauwels, L. (2000) 'Taking the Visual Turn in Research and Scholarly Communication: Key Issues in Developing a More Visually Literate (Social) Science', *Visual Sociology*, 15: 7–14.

Police Action Lawyers Group (2016) *Bach Commission on Access to Justice: Written Evidence from the Police Action Lawyers Group*, London: PALG.

Police Foundation (2009) *Politics and the Police: Oxford Policing Policy Forum*, London: Police Foundation.

Polk, O.E. and Armstrong, D.A. (2001) 'Higher Education and Law Enforcement Career Paths: Is the Road to Success Paved by Degree?', *Journal of Criminal Justice Education*, 12: 77–99.

Populus (2016) *Independent Police Complaints Commission: Stakeholder Feedback Study*, London: Populus.

Prenzler, T. and Porter, L. (2016) 'Improving Police Behaviour and Police–Community Relations through Innovative Responses to Complaints', in Lister, S. and Rowe, M. (eds) *Accountability of Policing*, London: Routledge, pp 49–68.

Procter, R., Crump, J., Karstedt, S., Voss, A. and Cantijoch, M. (2013) 'Reading the Riots: What Were the Police Doing on Twitter?', *Policing and Society*, 23: 413–36.

Punch, M. (2009) *Police Corruption*, Cullompton: Willan Publishing.

Putnam, R. (2001) *Bowling Alone: the Collapse and Revival of American Community*, New York: Simon and Schuster.

Ragnedda, M. (2017) *The Third Digital Divide: A Weberian Approach to Digital Inequalities*, London: Routledge.

Ratcliffe, J. (2002) 'Damned if You Don't, Damned if You Do: Crime Mapping and its Implications in the Real World', *Policing and Society*, 12: 211–25.

Rawlings, P. (2005) *Policing: A Short History*, Cullompton: Willan Publishing.

Reilly, P. (2015) 'Every Little Helps? YouTube, Sousveillance and the "antiTesco" riot in Stokes Croft', *New Media & Society*, 17: 755–71.

Reiner, R. (1985) 'Review of Controlling the Constable: Police Accountability in England and Wales, by T. Jefferson and R. Grimshaw', *The British Journal of Criminology*, 25: 296–98.

Reiner, R. (1991) *Chief Constables: Bobbies, Bosses or Bureaucrats?*, Oxford: Oxford University Press.

Reiner, R. (1992) 'Policing a Postmodern Society', *Modern Law Review*, 55: 761–78.

Reiner, R. (2000) *The Politics of the Police*, 3rd edn, Oxford: Oxford University Press.

Reiner, R. (2007) *Law and Order: An Honest Citizen's Guide to Crime and Control*, Cambridge: Polity.

Reiner, R. (2010) *The Politics of the Police*, 4th edn, Oxford: Oxford University Press.

Reiner, R. (2013) 'Who Governs? Democracy, Plutocracy, Science and Prophecy in Policing', *Criminology and Criminal Justice*, 13: 161–80.

Reiner, R. (2015) 'Revisiting the Classics: Three Seminal Founders of the Study of Policing: Michael Banton, Jerome Skolnick and Egon Bittner', *Policing and Society*, 25(3): 308–27.

Reiner, R. (2016) 'Power to the People? A Social Democratic Critique of the Coalition Government's Police Reforms', in Lister, S. and Rowe, M. (eds) *Accountability of Policing*, London: Routledge, pp. 132–49.

Reith, C. (1948) *A Short History of the British Police*, Oxford: Oxford University Press.

Richardson, A.V. (2017) 'Bearing Witness While Black: Theorizing African American Mobile Journalism after Ferguson', *Digital Journalism*, 5: 673–98.

Roberts, K. and Herrington, V. (2013) 'Organisational and Procedural Justice: A Review of the Literature and Its Implications for Policing', *Journal of Policing, Intelligence and Counter Terrorism*, 8: 115–30.

Romzek, B. and Dubnick, M. (1987) 'Accountability in the Public Sector: Lessons from the Challenger Tragedy', *Public Administration Review*, 47: 227–38.

Rosenbaum, D. (2007) 'The Limits of Hot Spots Policing', in Weisburd, D. and Braga, A.A. (eds) *Police Innovation: Contrasting Perspectives*, Cambridge: Cambridge University Press, pp. 245–65.

Rousseau, J.J. (1762/1968) *The Social Contract*, Harmondsworth: Penguin.

Rowe, M. (2004) *Policing, Race and Racism*, Cullompton: Willan Publishing.

Rowe, M. (2007) 'Rendering Visible the Invisible: Police Discretion, Professionalism and Ethics', *Policing and Society: An International Journal of Research and Policy*, 17: 279–94.

Rowe, M. and Hutton, F. (2012) '"Is your City Pretty Anyway?' Perspectives on Graffiti and the Urban Landscape', *Australian and New Zealand Journal of Criminology*, 45: 66–86.

Rowe, M. and Macauley, M. (2019) 'Giving Voice to the Victims of Sexual Assault: the Role of Police Leadership in Organisational Change', *Policing: an International Journal of Police Strategies & Management*, 42(3): 394–407.

Sandhu, A. (2017) '"I'm Glad that was on Camera": a Case Study of Police Officers' Perceptions of Cameras', *Policing and Society*, DOI: 10.1080/10439463.2017.1285917.

Sayer, A. (2014) *Why We Can't Afford the Rich*, Bristol: Policy Press.

Scarman, Lord (1981) *The Brixton Disorders*, London: HMSO.

Schein, E.H. (2010) *Organizational Culture and Leadership*, 4th edn, San Francisco: Jossey-Bass.

Schlembach, R. (2018) 'Undercover Policing and the Spectre of "Domestic Extremism": the Covert Surveillance of Environmental Activism in Britain', *Social Movement Studies*, 17(5): 491–506.

Scott, K. (2015) *'The Politics of the Police': Politicians and Policing in Scotland Today*, Scottish Institute for Policing Research, https://blog.dundee.ac.uk/sipr/2015/06/the-politics-of-the-police-politicians-and-policing-in-scotland-today/, accessed 7 August 2019.

Seyd, B. (2015) 'How Do Citizens Evaluate Public Officials? The Role of Performance and Expectations on Political Trust', *Political Studies*, 63: 73–90.

Shane, J. (2013) *Learning from Error in Policing – A Case Study in Organizational Accident Theory*, London: Springer.

Shearing, C.D. and Stenning, P.C. (1981) 'Modern Private Security: Its Growth and Implications', *Crime and Justice*, 3: 193–245.

Sherman, L.W. (1985) 'Becoming Bent: Moral Careers of Corrupt Policemen' in Elliston, F.A. and Feldberg, M. (eds) *Moral Issues in Police Work*, Totowa, New Jersey: Rowan and Allanheld.

Sherman, L.W. (2009) 'Evidence and Liberty: The Promise of Experimental Criminology', *Criminology & Criminal Justice*, 9(1): 5–28.

Sherman, L.W. (2013) 'The Rise of Evidence-Based Policing: Targeting, Testing, and Tracking', *Crime and Justice*, 42(1): 377–451.

Sherman, L.W. (2015) 'A Tipping Point for "Totally Evidenced Policing": Ten Ideas for Building an Evidence-Based Police Agency', *International Criminal Justice Review*, 25: 11–29.

Sherman, L.W., Schmidt, J.D., and Rogan, D.P. (1992) *Policing Domestic Violence: Experiments and Dilemmas*, New York: Free Press.

Skolnick, J. (1966) *Justice Without Trial*, New York: John Wiley & Sons.

Skolnick, J. (1991) 'It's not just a few rotten apples', *Los Angeles Times*, 7 March, Section B, Metro, p. 7.

Smith, G. (2003) 'Actions for Damages Against the Police and the Attitudes of Claimants', *Policing and Society*, 13: 413–22.

Smith, G. (2006) 'A Most Enduring Problem: Police Complaints Reform in England and Wales', *Journal of Social Policy*, 35: 121–41.

Solomos, J. (1988) *Black Youth, Racism and the State: the Politics of Ideology and Policy*, Cambridge: Cambridge University Press.

Sklansky, D.A. (2008) *Democracy and the Police*, Stanford: Stanford University Press.

Stenning, P. (2011) 'Governance of the Police: Independence, Accountability and Interference', *Flinders Law Journal*, 13: 241–67.

Stenson, K. (2002). 'Community Safety in Middle England: The Local Politics of Crime Control', in Hughes, G. and Edwards, A. (eds) *Crime Control and Community: The New Politics of Public Safety*, Cullompton: Willan Publishing, pp. 109–39.

Telep, C.W. and Somers, L.J. (2017) 'Examining Police Officer Definitions of Evidence-Based Policing: Are We Speaking the Same Language?', *Policing and Society: An International Journal of Research and Policy*, doi.org/10.1080/10439463.2017.1373775.

Thompson, G. (1991) *Markets, Hierarchies and Networks: the Coordination of Social Life*, London: Sage.

Topping, J. (2016) 'Accountability, Policing and the Police Service of Northern Ireland: Local Practices, Global Standards?' in Lister, S. and Rowe, M. (eds) *Accountability of Policing*, London: Routledge, pp. 150–71.

Torrible, C. (2016) 'Reconceptualising the Police Complaints Process as a Site of Contested Legitimacy Claims', *Policing and Society: An International Journal of Research and Policy*, DOI: 10.1080/10439463.2016.1191486.

van der Meer, T. (2017) 'Political Trust and the "Crisis of Democracy"', *Oxford Research Encyclopedias*, DOI: 10.1093/acrefore/9780190228637.013.77.

Verschoor, M. (2018) 'The Democratic Boundary Problem and Social Contract Theory', *European Journal of Political Theory*, 17: 3–22.

Vice (2014) 'Cities Are Using Hidden Webs of Acoustic Sensors to Detect Gunfire', https://motherboard.vice.com/en_us/article/xywgva/cities-are-using-hidden-webs-of-acoustic-sensors-to-detect-gunfire, accessed 27 April 2018.

Waddington, P.A.J. (1994) *Liberty and Order: Policing Public Order in a Capital City*, London: UCL Press.

Waddington, P.A.J. (1999) *Policing Citizens: Authority and Rights*, London: UCL Press.

Waghorn, N.J. (2016) 'Watching the Watchmen: Resisting Drones and the "Protestor Panoptican"', *Geographica Helvetica*, 71: 99–108.

Wakefield, A. (2003) *Selling Security*, Cullompton: Willan.

Wall, D.S. (1998) *The Chief Constables of England and Wales: The Socio-Legal History of a Criminal Justice Elite*, Aldershot: Ashgate.

Wells, H. (2016) 'PCCs, Roads Policing and the Dilemmas of Increased Democratic Accountability', *British Journal of Criminology*, 56: 274–92.

Westley, W. (1953) 'Violence and the Police', *American Journal of Sociology*, 59: 34–41.

Westmarland, L. (2000) 'Telling the Truth the Whole Truth and Nothing but the Truth? Ethics and the Enforcement of Law', *Journal of Ethical Sciences and Services*, 2(3), 193–202.

Westmarland, L. (2005) 'Police Ethics and Integrity. Breaking the Blue Code of Silence', *Policing and Society: An International Journal of Research and Policy*, 15: 145–65.

Westmarland, L. (2013), 'Snitches Get Stitches: Homicide Investigation in Downtown DC', *Policing and Society*, 23: 311–27.

Westmarland, L. and Rowe, M. (2018) 'Police Ethics and Integrity: Can a New Code Overturn the Blue Code?', *Policing and Society: An International Journal of Research and Policy*, 28: 854–70.

White, A. (2012) 'The New Political Economy of Private Security', *Theoretical Criminology*, 16: 85–101.

White, A. (2016) 'Private Security and the Politics of Accountability' in Lister, S. and Rowe, M. (eds) *Accountability of Policing*, London: Routledge, pp. 172–91.

Whitfield, J. (2004) *Unhappy Dialogue: The Metropolitan Police and Black Londoners in Post-War Britain*, Cullompton: Willan.

Wilkinson, R.G. and Pickett, K. (2009) *The Spirit Level: Why More Equal Societies Almost Always Do Better*, London: Allen Lane.

Wood, D.A. (2016) 'The Importance of Liberal Values within Policing: Police and Crime Commissioners, Police Independence and the Spectre of Illiberal Democracy', *Policing and Society*, 26: 148–64.

Wood, J. and Shearing, C. (2007) *Imagining Security*, Cullompton: Willan Publishing.

Workman-Stark, A. (2017) *Inclusive Policing from the Inside Out*, Ottawa: Springer.

Yarwood, R. (2015) 'Lost and Hound: The More-than-Human Networks of Rural Policing', *Journal of Rural Studies*, 39: 278–87.

Young, J. (1999) *The Exclusive Society: Social Exclusion, Crime and Difference in Late Modernity*, London: Sage.

Young, M. (1991) *An Inside Job: Policing and Police Culture in Britain*, Oxford: Clarendon Press.

Zhu, K., He, X., Xiang, B., Zhang, L. and Pattavina, A. (2016) 'How Dangerous Are Your Smartphones? App Usage Recommendation with Privacy Preserving', *Mobile Information Systems*, doi:10.1155/2016/6804379.

Zietwitz, M. (2016) 'Governing Algorithms: Myth, Mess, and Methods', *Science, Technology, and Human Values*, 41: 3–16.

Index